The Woodstock Sandal and Further Steps

The Woodstock Sandal
and Further Steps

Charles Cantalupo

AFRICA WORLD PRESS

TRENTON | LONDON | CAPE TOWN | NAIROBI | ADDIS ABABA | ASMARA | IBADAN | NEW DELHI

AFRICA WORLD PRESS
541 West Ingham Avenue | Suite B
Trenton, New Jersey 08638

Book design: Dawid Kahts
Cover art: Painting by Alicia Kiah Cantalupo
Cover design: Ashraful Haque

Cataloging-in-Publication Data may be obtained from the Library of Congress.

ISBNs: 978-1-56902-712-7 (HB)
       978-1-56902-713-4 (PB)

Contents

Foreword

The Prelude

didst thou, beauteous Stream,
Make ceaseless music through the night and day
Which with its steady cadence, tempering
Our human waywardness, compos'd my thoughts....

William Wordsworth

There is a ubiquitous joke among the former citizens of Woodstock Nation, sufficiently pervasive to find its way into Charles Cantalupo's poem, to the effect that if you remember Woodstock, you surely were not there. I wasn't there, though it haunted my youth. A dear friend who had once worked for a small radio station in Emporium, Pennsylvania, proudly carried his Woodstock Press Pass in his wallet for decades, though that and all other passes became wholly superfluous on the first day of the festival. All rock festivals are alike, though each is alike in its own distinctive way, and every rock festival since has borne the burden of comparison to that urfestival of the festive. Thanks to Altamont, our collective memory has decided that the Age of Aquarius died a-borning, leaving hippiedom among the most short-lived of cultural phenomena. The Beat had edged into the Beatles, and the next thing we knew Punk was already rattling its bars and spitting on the grave of

Prog Rock. You had to be there, we say to puzzled youth, but in fact you need not have been there at all. Most weren't.

But this poet was.

And by the evidence of this collection, poems with a distinguished record of publication already, the youthful Charles Cantalupo was even then thinking along the lines that give us these lines. "Songs I composed, but I didn't write," he writes. Like me, he came out of high school in a band. Unlike me, indeed unlike almost anybody in those days except the Byrds-obsessed, he was playing an electric twelve string. Which should give us pause. Near the end, closer to the now, he advises, "I call it 'minor heroic,' and write dactylic hexameters." Twice six gets you twelve. I call it "bent formalism." Much as we bend a note, he bends the form. I imagine this resulted in many a broken string along the way ("some scintillations in a long poem"), but, as it was for Wordsworth, it's all about the journey. "What a long, strange trip it's been," wrote The Grateful Dead just seven years after Woodstock Nation had begun to fall apart into disparate states and statelessness. Most of this verse is organized around central moments, conceits, charged details. "John is like Woodstock to me" might be unexpected, even if we pause to reread Mark 1:7 before going on with the poem. But John the Baptist (and here I note that I was raised among the Baptists) spent his time in the wilderness. We Baptists called him "John the Immerser," and though this poetry is both more Catholic and catholic than that, it's clear that the poet underwent a total immersion and rose a different man.

More than once, hence the repeated unstrapping of sandals marking the stages of what might have been a *Künstlerroman* had the poet been a novelist; what we have is a sort of roaming Romanist, one who has slipped the moorings and set out across the cultural landscape of the past half century and more. We follow the meters through our history, as Cantalupo finds himself taking a turning, both aesthetically and ideologically, here described as, "Part of a process between iconoclasm and icon." Much as in an earlier poem, Frank O'Hara's lunch took a turn when LeRoi Jones arrived with the news that the police had beaten Miles Davis in the street the night before, this pilgrim's progress tracks its movements by the interruptions of radio news: "Somebody named Leroi Jones, a poet, had been arrested." Like the best poets, the turnings in life and history are often underlined by turnings in the verse. This is particularly effective in "At the Grave of H.D.," in my reading one of the strongest passages of this book. Here the youth who went in search of the lost chord finds his way to meter-making argument: "'[F]ollowing intricate song's lost measure.' Following. Measure. / Intricate. Song. But why lost? Lost? Is it? I say 'Greek flower.'"

We follow the poems and the poet across to Europe, to Palestine, to Africa. Cantalupo arrives in an actual Africa with the Africa of Joseph Conrad trailing along. But it's Conrad's Africa as confronted by Chinua Achebe's. I've always held that Marlowe wasn't lying when he told the Beloved that Kurtz's last word was her name. Generations of readers were just looking for the horror in all the wrong places. The poem inhabits a moment before translation, "which never happens," asks about an ever-receding Renaissance, "When what the African woman doesn't say in Conrad's story / Finally begins to be heard." This is, I think, a mode of Walter Benjamin's messianism without a messiah. A West that thought of Africa as one of those blank places on the map, that thought of the African woman as a silent, blank darkness, is the same West that thinks of Africa as "shithole countries." That Africa existed only in the mind of the white West, which was part of Achebe's critique.

Ngũgĩ wa Thiong'o and Eritrea would seem distant from Woodstock Nation, but we are told all the time, it's a small world after all. And if the Kenyan writer was, at the very least, premature in declaring the language question in Africa settled once and for all, Cantalupo's springing measures bring us word of a more capacious wording, reopen the questions of language, find new harmonic structures for the lost chord, bring us back again and again to our lost / found nation.

Aldon Lynn Nielsen

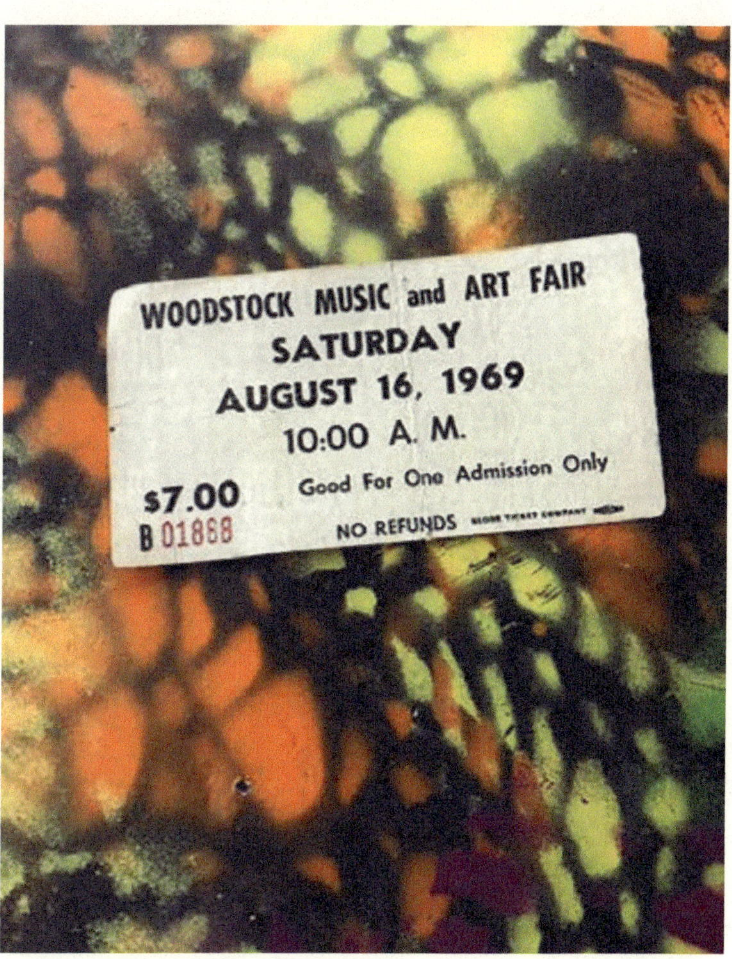

WOODSTOCK MUSIC and ART FAIR
SATURDAY
AUGUST 16, 1969
10:00 A. M.
Good For One Admission Only
$7.00
B 01868
NO REFUNDS

The Woodstock Sandal

I see a sandal of many sandals, the Woodstock sandal.

What did I know when I graduated West Orange High School:
June 1969, raised in suburbs of Newark, New Jersey?
I would start Washington U in fall but gave it little thought.
Playing electric guitar, a twelve string; my band, Spring Fever;
Surfing and swim team and girlfriends mattered much more
     than college.
Songs I composed, but I didn't write – or like literature.
School gave us Hemingway and Fitzgerald, seeming so tame
     and
Obvious when we compared them to the Beatles' lyrics in
Songs on *Revolver* and *Sgt. Pepper's Lonely Hearts Club Band*,
Or to the words sounding psychedelic in Cream and Hendrix.
Reading "The Waste Land," I liked it and not understanding,
     but
Tweed jackets, button-down shirts, and short hair couldn't
     compare with
Paisleys and Day-Glos and long hair, wearing beads and bell
     bottoms:
High school rock stardom and totally derivative…and yet
It seemed original at the time and who would not want to
Act and explode like the Who or be so cool and stoned as the
Jefferson Airplane and sing forever, "Somebody to Love?"

Several nights after graduation, as we played the song
Badly for two drunks who nodded in a Union City bar
Not quite as bad as the street outside where their friend beat his
     wife,
I comprehended the Fillmore East, where I heard all the groups
Who did the songs on our play list, was too far, though five
     minutes
Over the Hudson and down on Second in the East Village.
I'd rather be there to see and hear my favorites playing
All their incredible music live instead of my doing
Second-rate covers of greatest hits already played to death.
Therefore, I quit my band and got tickets for the night after
To hear the super group, Blind Faith, play their first New York
     concert:
Clapton and Baker and Winwood – gods who would play
     together,
And I would be there in Madison Square Garden with my girl.
Anyway, I knew I'd quit Spring Fever, leave for St. Louis –
Wherever that was – and go to college, soon in September.
Why shouldn't I have a far-out summer? Also, I heard that
Some of my high school friends who loved music, but not in the
     band,
Wanted to go to some music festivals, and so did I,
Joining them in a red '63 VW bus for
Newport on Fourth of July. Atlantic City Pop came next,
Early in August, and later that month we went to Woodstock.

Read in the Gospel of Mark, 1:7. John the Baptist says,
"Someone is following me…who is more powerful than I….
I am not fit to kneel…and undo the strap of his sandals."
John speaks ironically, since he's more than "fit" as a prophet,
Which it's assumed all his readers know, and most of all Jesus.
John is like Woodstock to me, and so is my life after that:
 All of it undoes a sandal, then I put another on:

This one, then that one, then this one – always another
Sandal to wear. When there's not? I'm gone. No mystery is
        there.
College and grad school, profession, more and different music,
Travel to Europe, and writing, art and literature, sex,
Love, and my first meeting death and going back to religion,
Travel to Africa, love come back and so much more, marriage,
Children, and aging – they all create who I am beyond the
Festivals held in the Woodstock summer, 1969.
Still they were more than "fit to…undo the strap of" what I
        knew
For so much more to know and its power: not mere suburban
High school experience…and the play lists of Spring Fever,
Seeming immortal or not. The Newport, Atlantic City,
And Woodstock festivals made the spectacle of change and
Surge of excitement the key to what I've wanted ever since:
Consciously strapping and then unconsciously undoing the
Strap on my thinking: on where to go and what I've wanted to
Do for the last fifty years; my putting on and taking off
One sandal after another. Call it the Woodstock sandal.

All of the sandals, the strapping and unstrapping disappear
For this one sandal when Woodstock friends and I hang out
        again.
Moments from back then return, undying, self-possessed,
        unchanged:
Joined and secured to their music, still the same, of course, as
        then.
Even Spring Fever, though now called Holme, plays much the
        same set lists:
Down the shore, Jersey's best bar band, and they also own the
        bar.
Joy in the present not mere nostalgia makes me imagine
I could be playing there with them or be listening with friends:

Peggy and Judy and Robin, Ken and Bruce; pushing seventy
Rather than seventeen yet beginning before beginning
And everlasting…but back then who would bother to say it?
Certainly, I wouldn't nor expect that soon out of nowhere
I'd see the strap on that scene undone and hopelessly mortal,
As it seems now only after one or two hours' retelling,
Wearing the sandal of many sandals – the Woodstock sandal.
"Are you experienced" was the question and the famous song
Hendrix recorded in '67. Clearly, I wasn't,
Not till the festivals, and I don't mean "stoned" or "beautiful:"
Answers that Hendrix himself sings as he fades out the
        soundtrack,
Playing the lead and the rhythm, A-flat octaves, and backwards.
Yet the experience, not the music of the festivals,
Made the song true to life or, at least, the way I would follow:

"From the Sky," 1969, Barry Z Levine, © Barry Z Levine, www.woodstockwitness.com.

Not merely hearing what I'd heard countless times on radio
And on the portable KLH, the stereo record
Player I had at home in my bedroom: the experience;
Going and being there: shocked by what I'd never seen before;
What I was missing and needed whether I knew it or not.
More of a commonplace than a revelation, I admit.
Only I never got over it. "Are you experienced"
Like a refrain yet in many, changing forms won't go away.
"Undo the strap" like a chorus ultimately has its say.
Starting with Woodstock, I've had more sandals seeing better
     days.
Sandals of who I am…but back to the original pair.

Packed in the van from New Jersey, heading to the Newport
     Jazz
Festival, we didn't care about the jazz, barely knowing
Names like Art Blakey, Miles Davis, Herbie Hancock,
     Bill Evans –
Certainly, we never listened to them. We wanted to hear
Rock groups the festival for the first time that year included,
To the jazz purists' dismay, who saw it as abandonment;
And they were right in a way: that is, our self-abandonment;
Out of our mind, psychedelic total listening pleasure.
Is it embarrassing now, such stultifying ignorance?
Yes, my obliviousness: the precondition realized
First at the festivals and repeatedly ever since then:
"Ignorance was my first teacher, yet I knew I didn't know."
Quotes around that mean it took me decades, many more
     sandals
Later to know it and write it, trying to understand why
Being in Africa for the first time shattered my calm of
Euro-American isolation I vowed to uphold –
Also embarrassing now? Of course, and how many other

Times I've not known when I should know, and they've made
    me change for the
Better, or so I believe is the life of the mind to love?

Blood, Sweat, and Tears, Ten Years After, Jeff Beck, Led
    Zeppelin, and
Sly and the Family Stone – I never dreamed twelve months later
I wouldn't listen to rock again for the next fifteen years
But to the very musicians I had hated at Newport.
Joining the legions of Coltrane devotees, I would commute
From Jersey suburbs to city jazz clubs, enthralled by Davis,
Evans, and Hancock, and McCoy Tyner, wow Pharoah
    Sanders….
Changing the music, however, didn't change the excitement
It made me feel from what I felt at the Newport festival
Or at the festivals that soon followed…or now when I hear
"…alles Fleish, es ist wie Gras," in October – Brahms's *Requiem*;
Or when I go to the Philly Orchestra and hear it play
His or some other composer's absolutely life-changing
Symphony like a religious vision or experience.
Then again moving from pop to jazz to classical with age
Also is commonplace – less so, maybe, after Woodstock's time.
Nevertheless, then and now, its Dionysian power
Comes back, undoing the strap of what I'm thinking was
    enough
For something no less intense and radical but different.
Jefferson Airplane, the Who, the Rolling Stones, Jimi Hendrix
Meet my new Woodstock in Arvo Pärt, Steve Reich, John
    Tavener,
John Luther Adams, John Adams, David Lang, so many more.
Maybe the festivals' music has paled, if not the feeling
It could inspire but, again, I go back: the experience
Made all the difference – not so much the music I knew well.
I mean what I didn't know before I got there mattered most.

Parked in a little league field, we camped at Newport, squeezed
    between
Guys who had set up a smoky camp with their motorcycles
Like a stockade; and a beat-up school bus painted with flowers,
Planets, a Yin Yang, and crazy birds amidst big, swirling stars.
Since I forgot to bring food, I ate for free on the bus and
Watched a spontaneous jam played by a group called The Fugs:
Banned from the festival for obscenity but a perfect
Match for the gang with their motorcycles letting us listen
For all the gallons of Gallo port wine we had in the van.
Nor did we need the stuff, we soon realized after we arrived,
Visited by a nice guy who called himself, "Dr. Drugs" – or
Maybe we gave him that name, who can remember exactly? –
Selling for cheap any psychedelic drug that existed,
Money back guaranteed if it wasn't safe…and no bad trips.
Nobody worried. Why should we, laughing, laughing and
    amazed?
Hog Farm, a longstanding hippie commune from California
Came with the bus and would offer food and security, too,
Later at Woodstock. Unwittingly, I followed in their tow.

For "jazz aficionados," Newport's festival got us
Plus twenty thousand more people like us, only there for rock.
Not buying tickets, we herded on a hill overlooking
Gates and a ten-foot high fence around the seating and the
    stage.
Mulligan, Brubeck, Art Blakey, Burton, rain…. Nobody cared.
Bring us the young group from San Francisco. We want Sly and
    the
Family Stone, and they burst out shouting their album song.
    "Stand!
Don't you know…you are free…if you want to be….
    Everybody

Stand!" To be free the crowd rushed the stage. The rain and
    firecrackers
Burst around gate crashers climbing over fences and falling
Under the clubs of the cops who waited on the other side,
Throwing them back until all the fences finally came down.
Searchlight trucks drove up, illuminating some kind of battle.
Sly sang the anthem. "I want to take you…Higher!" The crowd
    sang,
"Higher!" It screamed back and forth. It echoed, "Higher,"
    louder and
Louder and all that we wanted: get out of control "Higher!"
Hillside in Newport, an intimation: unstrap the sandal.

Sly and his group being black – although he had white sidemen,
    too –
Black jazz musicians, and Hendrix black – I didn't notice it.
Race and the struggle for civil rights: Dubois' "problem of the
Twentieth century" seemed important, but it still left me
All but oblivious to reality beyond music's
Sometimes expressing it. Yet the era's other worst issue,
Fighting the Vietnam war, seemed less significant, too, than
Music relating the conflict to the world and the artist.
Now the experience of the riots seems most important –
Whatever music I heard or didn't hear at the Newport
Festival – since they connected me, although subconsciously,
To the Newark riots in '67, just a few miles from
Where I lived, "up the hill," in West Orange: where the
    rebellion
Seemed far away: the four days of burning down and looting
    Newark:
Blacks against local police backed up by the National Guard.
Twenty-six people died. Hundreds injured. Property
    destroyed.
Close geographically, in the suburbs we were worlds away.

Sly Stone, Sly and the Family Stone, August 16, 1969. Photo by Joe Sia, wolfgangs.com.

9 | The Woodstock Sandal

Sorry if I was so ignorant (again) or half sorry.
Writing about what I've learned instead of making myself seem
As if I knew what I didn't gets to why I write my story:
Part of a process between iconoclasm and icon.
Suddenly part of the Newport riot narrowed the distance,
Even a little and unperceivable. I remember
On the first night of the riots, how I found out about them.
After my father and I had dinner at an old Jewish
Deli in Orange, a town between the city and suburbs,
We had to walk to his 1964 aquamarine
Galaxy parked a few blocks away, when I saw army Jeeps
Driving towards Newark. We got in the car, turned on the
        radio,
And as we drove up the hill the local news reported that
Somebody named Leroi Jones, a poet, had been arrested,
Charged with inciting the riots, and in custody in Newark.
Born there, Dad fled when the blacks began to outnumber the
        whites.
Most of them did – my friends' fathers, too: Jews, Irish, Italian,
German, whatever. They worked in Newark and drove away at
        night.
Many American cities suffered similar white flight.
Rarely if ever I heard my father curse, but he believed –
Based on his being raised in a big Italian immigrant
Family and now a lawyer in the Essex County court –
Blacks ruined Newark, and he swore out loud at the latest
        report.
Tell me a fatuous concert riot undoes a sandal
Civil and national violent unrest left tightly strapped?

May 1970, ten months after Newport, another
Rioting crowd I'm in wants to burn down the ROTC
Building at Washington University, and I'm cheering.

Rocks shower down and the windows shatter. Students I don't
    know
Kick out the doors of the Quonset hut: the screaming and
    sirens
Perfectly timed for more students getting bolder and running
Up to the windows and door to get inside and to light fires.
Seeing police cars and firetrucks and the students around me
Reaching down and throwing rocks at them, I want a rock, too,
    but
Better to run, I think. Sprinting through the fields behind my
    dorm,
Maybe I see a state trooper running after me before
Finally, I'm in my room. I tear down the American
Flag that I hung in my window as a protest to the war.
Now I'm afraid that my decoration might draw attention
Where I hide under my bed: my Woodstock sandal fallen off
Back in the field somewhere? I don't know. I'd get another one.

Early in August, nine months before, Atlantic City Pop
Festival closed with another huge crowd close to rioting.
Happily, I was a part of it and totally enthralled.
Close to the stage, we saw Janis Joplin and her new blues
    band –
After she broke up her psychedelic rock group, Big Brother.
"Try (Just a Little Bit Harder)" now had more early-60s
Soul sound and funk with less forlorn wailing and a lot more
    dance.
Not that my friends or I realized this or cared, at least not me.
Close to the stage we could almost feel her shaking and
    sweating –
Music induced, drugs or booze, but heroin? We never dreamed.
Primary, I should say primal, was her being a woman.
Music came second. Like Sly at Newport: the experience.
Not at the time, I admit, but now in retrospect I have

No better or more specific memory of the music
Than I can easily find on YouTube or on Spotify.

Joplin had ended, exhausted – like the band and the crowd, too.
Time to leave – all of us thought this had to be the finale –
When a new set of musicians, black and dressed in tuxedos
Started emerging onstage and lined up ready to perform.
Who they were nobody seemed to know, and I can't remember,
Still I can picture they started playing low, tight R & B.
What I saw next defied my imagination: someone black
Half pranced and half slunk across the stage and to the very
    edge.

Who was this dressed in a huge white fur coat: taking it off and
Offering it like a sacrificial totem to the crowd,

Pete Townshend, The Who, 1969, Stephen Goldblatt asc bsc. 2.

Spellbound one late muggy summer night on a racetrack
     infield?
Who was this…woman? No. It was Little Richard, and the
     horde
Started to celebrate, heaving towards the stage, out of control;
Knocking me down, but I pulled myself up, grabbing a
     stranger.
All of us worshipped: ecstatic, born again for this new god,
Suddenly joined by the goddess, Janis Joplin, to perform.

"We got to Woodstock," as Joni Mitchell sang, "half a million
Strong," though she wasn't there. Frankly, I recall very little,
Like the stale joke that to really be there meant remembering
Nothing at all. But my friends remember more, when I ask
     them,
Nor is it pastoral like what Mitchell wrote. I will confess:
Too many sandals unstrapped and strapped since then blur
     most details.
Back to the lyrics: she gets what Woodstock and the other two
Festivals did for me then and ever since; hearing the verse
"[m]aybe the time of year… / Or…the time of man" to
     recognize
"I don't know who I am / But you know life is for learning" like
"Are you experienced" echoed in the words, "Undo the strap,"
As I remember the summer when I did for the first time:
Lifetimes ago but a kind of archetype for what followed.
Draping my stray details and my random experiences
On this original form, I don't need much more about it.
Movies, recordings, and books or many online resources
Fill in the rest but these images, at least, I can salvage:
Daltry's white fringe suit and Townsend's leaps to pinwheel
     power chords;
Open tuned, fast strumming Havens; Cocker's spastic
     gyrations;

One of my friends in the bad trip tent…the nurse stroking his
    hand;
Traffic-jammed roads through the woods where we walk
    unsuspectingly;
Blankets on mud and the wreaking watermelon rinds sliding
One foot an hour towards the stage; my hearing and barely
    caring
Hendrix's guitar solo ricochets "The Star-Spangled Banner"
While I walk totally wasted in the early morning air
Back to the tent after other famous rock groups played all night.

Whether the festivals, Woodstock their synecdoche, signaled
Some kind of paradigm shift in culture or in history:
With any certainty, I can't say but, personally, "yes."
Moving beyond the received conventions I was taught or not;
Forced to confront what I had not thought of or experienced;
Letting myself be disoriented; status quo unstrapped;
Any such openness in my life began at Woodstock and
It set my pattern of willingness to change ever since then.
As for affecting the nation and the world, look at headlines
Yesterday or today and tomorrow: poverty, sickness,
Violence, war, and injustice; evil is as prevalent,
As it was then. Is it more? Consider social progress like
Civil rights, women's rights, LGBT rights, and other signs
Not of hate but of love for humanity in the US
And in the influence of this aspect of American
Culture since Woodstock, the Woodstock spirit. Let me say,
    "Amen."
Let it be more faith than knowledge. Let it. Hundreds of
    flowers….

After the festival, maybe a week later, I started
College at Washington University in Missouri.
Me in the back and my parents in the front seat of our Ford,

Driving on campus the first time, when we found the dorm, I
    saw
Students who looked like they came right from the festival:
    lanky,
Long haired, disheveled, and stoned. At Dad's "they don't look
    like students,"
I only said, "They look cool." St. Louis felt like my new home,
For a lot longer than Woodstock, yet my parents dropped me
    off:
Innocent and instrumental in a metamorphosis.
Change and intensity; counter culture like I never knew:
I was prepared for the unexpected incongruity,
Or so I thought, and embraced it, maybe too familiarly,
Making new friends who thought college seemed like another
    Woodstock.
When did I recognize that another sandal had to drop?
Eight months of classes or two semesters later when I hid
Under the bed in my dorm room after running away from
Joining the students who burned down campus ROTC and
Started attacking police and firemen, little did I know
Losing a sandal in panic meant I would not get caught yet –
Stuck in my literal Woodstock mindset as it came apart.
Hearing the word "moratorium" applied to "end the war,"
How it related to Vietnam at first, I had no clue.
Songs that protested the war were common: in fact, I wrote one
Back in eighth grade and performed it often. "Together and
    Pray"
Was a big hit at the junior high assembly, and it made
Me want to write more songs: so I got my start as a poet.
Later a record producer, Ernie Susser, recorded
Spring Fever doing the song in his not quite state-of-the-art
Studio in the Weequahaic section of Philip Roth Newark.
Promising teach-ins about the war, the moratorium
Didn't compare, but it cancelled classes, which I had to like.

Better to play "got to revolution," Airplane's new album
Called *Volunteers*. As a major in political science,
I would be "dancing down…streets…come on" and "marching
    to the sea."
Woodstock would go to war with the uniformed state police
    and
National guardsmen patrolling campus – whatever that meant:
War at home ending the war in Vietnam – or wherever.
Then came the actual gunning down of students at Kent State.

"Four [students} dead in Ohio" led to music by Crosby
Stills, Nash & Young that I listened to on earphones in my
    room.
Two more dead in Mississippi: shot by cops at Jackson State.
Passionate music for murdered students was the life for me.
One night I pictured Mom walking in, and I wouldn't know her.
I saw a sandal of many sandals, the Woodstock sandal.
What would I not undo? It would take the Woodstock sandal,
    too.
Not that I knew this then. Many years passed, and I wouldn't
    know
Wearing the sandal of Woodstock meant it had to be
    transformed
Over and over again and each time had to be undone.

Then I read Dante's *Inferno* in Ciardi's translation –
Nonstop until *Purgatorio* and *Paradiso* fell.
Dante's *Commedia*, later called divine, struck me like God.
Protest, affirm, and compose word music in *terza rima*.
State your religion, tradition, individuality,
History, and your philosophy: a mystical vision
Moving the sun and the stars with love and poetry's power.
Jersey suburbia, summer music festivals, campus
War to the soundtracks of rock and roll, the searching for spirit

Woodstock, 1969, Baron Wolman, Photo © Baron Wolman.

17 | The Woodstock Sandal

Only in Eastern religions…all went puff and had to go:
All of them no more than "Pleasant Valley Sunday(s)" Carole
     King
Wrote about when she lived in West Orange in the late 60s.
Sorry, but nothing compared with Dante, and nothing came
     close.
Therefore, I vowed to learn my own Western culture entirely –
Not any other before – and I swam free of the Beats and
Radical leftism; Asia and Black Nationalism;
Even American lit, I figured, pre-1900:
Hadn't my grandparents immigrated to America
After that? I was a European. Book me a ticket.
Let me be fit to kneel and undo this sandal's strap anew.

Spirit of Woodstock go with me. College in Canterbury
Seemed like the perfect first destination. Studying Shakespeare
With the cathedral just down the hill, my daily pilgrimage,
Felt as intense and life-changing as the festival music
Crowds. I remember a British student demonstration with
Stones' music; "Sympathy for the Devil," played like a movie.
I didn't care. I was leaving on a bus bound for Dover,
Where I would crawl through the lush and sheep shit fields out
     to a cliff.
King Lear IV:6 and lines 12 to 25 – called "Shakespeare's Cliff."
Reading and looking down I checked the description by Edgar:
"…dizzy…so low… / crows and choughs that wing the
     midway air /…way down."
Studying English, I quested to become literature.
Outside of Keswick, I found a hillside much too steep to climb.
Therefore, I went down on hands and knees to crawl up the
     loose shale,
Sure I would find a view no one else saw in the Lake District.
Goodbye to jeans and my tie-dye shirts for Harris tweeds and
     caps

(Keeping my shoulder-length hair). I'd make Keats's letters my
    sacred
Text at all times in my pocket. I'd write like Edmund Spenser.
What could be better than drinking wine and reading *Faerie
    Queene*?
Luckily coal miners went on strike. Resulting power cuts
Led to no heat and no lights: the perfect time to spend hours
Wearing my ultimate camo – my new British accent – and
Writing in candlelit Canterbury's holy cathedral.
Clearly the content changed. But the impetus remained the
    same:
Seeing what I didn't know and wanted to experience;
Nothing like what I had ever seen before brought another
Woodstock-like festival meltdown and a rebirth I embraced.
Machault, Firenze, *The Prelude*, Chartres, Siena, Duccio,
Paris, the Louvre, Monteverdi, Nietzsche: where did they come
    from?
Where did the Airplane, the Dead, the Who, Sly Stone, and
    Hendrix go?
London to Amsterdam, Rome, Milan, Palermo and Athens:
They were my news, as Pound told me: maybe old, but they
    stayed news.
Reveling like a young Edward Casaubon, whom I'd heard of,
Not reading *Middlemarch* yet, I thought that's it: truth and
    beauty.
Not just a weekend, a three-day music festival, BA,
MA, or getting a PhD: this storming and raiding
High Western culture continued strapping me for fifteen years –
All the way to my becoming a professor in English,
Rooted in Woodstock and all that summer's total amazement.
Meanwhile the roads throughout Europe that I traveled
    constantly –
Kerry to Athos, perhaps predictably, all led to Rome:
Back to the faith I was baptized in through quattrocento and

Trecento visions; enthralled like I was on that Newport hill,
Or on a South Jersey racetrack's infield hearing two gods sing,
Only now Duccio's altarpiece, the *Maestá* held me.

Nothing analogous to a strapped or unstrapped sandal hit
Me in the mid-1980s; cancer slaughtered my young wife.
Only my festival of high Western art, literature,
Music, and poetry kept me going like nothing happened,
And they were worthy to kneel and unstrap any mystery.
Really – except I took one more step, and it seemed forward
        then.
Not only back to my faith through art, but what if through my
        faith
Into new art yet an art of hope to go with Paul's saying,
"Hope that is seen is not hope," in Romans, verse 8:24?
Art could be seen, if not hope, in Christianity and God,
Yet I was seeing hope, too, if I could make the connection.
Not that it all hadn't been thrown out in history before.
I wanted poems to root in Catholic theology:
Difficult, learned, and deep, and my alternative theory
To Derrida and Foucault.   I fell for Teilhard de Chardin
In a weak moment but mostly read the fathers of the Church:
Augustine, Benedict, Bernard of Clairvaux were my Woodstock.
I found a house in the woods near a Cistercian priory.
Living alone I could walk there every day for morning Mass –
Praying and singing from huge, illuminated psalters and
Best of all it was in Latin, not a word of English or
Rancorous sermons on women, gays, and stopping abortion.
Hiking for hours alone revealed enough morality.
Also, I wanted to root more deeply in the images
Fueled by language I worshipped in to set my mind on fire.
Where did they come from, and who first made the
        iconography?
Christ, Virgin Mary, the Holy Spirit, saints and disciples:

Where did the pictures originate, and could I go to the
Sinai Peninsula monastery of St. Catherine's,
Where I'd behold the first icons ever made, supposedly?
Hoping to find affirmation there, I did, not suspecting
It would begin a much longer trip than what I was planning:
Very much opposite the direction where I thought I went,
Losing a sandal again, again without my knowing then.

Fittingly going with one of my old friends from long ago
Woodstock days (irony I was unaware of at the time,
And he still listened to much of the same music from back
    then),
We flew to Israel – picking up the festival spirit
Where we left off; plus his being Jewish – we had a great time
At his Bar Mitzvah – meant he knew the Old Testament while I
Back being Catholic identified what came out of the New;
All of which we were amazed to see came out of real places.
Piety, nevertheless, had limits. We liked partying:
Driving around the West Bank especially. It was safe,
Open, and welcoming – hardly any Israeli soldiers;
Muslims and Jews coexisting; throw in Christians, with us, too.
Frankly, my fervency for new revelations seemed to fade.
Friendship and pleasures of old took over to renew as much.
Maybe in retrospect that's what made the Holy Sepulchre
Not overwhelming; the same for icons and St. Catherine's,
Bethlehem, Nablus, the tomb of Joseph; Hebron's half-a-day
Temple and half-a-day mosque, the Cave of the Patriarchs,
    where
Down in a hole through the floor an echo, lower and lower,
Higher to God – yet the feeling of some strange, new festival
Leading to something forbidden but by whom and granted
    when?
Some kind of thunder had rumbled, but no lightning strikes or
    rain:

Certainly not on the road to take a swim in the Dead Sea;
Stopping in Jericho first to take a look provoked the storm.
Call it a whirlwind, a vortex, out of nowhere suddenly,
All but invisibly, with no outward sign, and in my mind.
Who was I, standing in sand where twenty cities disappeared?
Sun glaring mirrored the Dead Sea straight ahead and blinded
    me,
Only to see to the north deserted camps for refugees
And to the south spiny cliffs of Qumran like a killing spree.
Tunneling ants in the sand around me dug infinity.
All of the holiest icons I saw in St. Catherine's,
All of the sacred sites where I worshipped throughout Israel,
And all my life to this moment knelt and undid my sandal.
None of what I wanted mattered like the unknown I felt here.

Then I recovered. We flew to Cairo, for some more good times.
Jericho could be an aberration, and I repressed it,
Booked in a palace that dated back to the Suez Canal's
Opening under the French before the British took over.
Not that I cared about Egypt and colonialism,
Even if I had the chance, caught up immediately in
Chaos that ruled Cairo's streets, or so they seemed when I went
    out.
Making my way to the National Museum for its art,
I sensed the Jericho shadows and the ants closing back in.
Nothing prepared me, again, for where I was: not fifteen years
Writing devoutly of my own Western culture – that's for sure.
I could have been on the verge of saying this to myself then,
If the museum's calm entrance didn't take away my fears,
Fooling myself into saying, "OK. Ready to go in – "
Not even close, the suburban sheltered seventeen-year old
Boy at a festival going wild for rock and roll star songs
Fell into politics burning children's minds for foreign wars
He could escape behind walls of books like heaven on earth and
Join with his own for all time until he had to see love die,

Once and for all. So I tumbled room to room and floor to floor
Into the black and gold angles, glittering in uncanny
Details and symbols with infinite perspective and strange gods
Where I could only be disconnected and ephemeral,
Lost in the images and the messages of another
Jericho, but the museum let me dig my own tunnels
Back into what I had missed and, therefore, couldn't recognize.
Leaving the place in a panic of desire but mystified
How I could want what I'd never understand, I didn't know
What else to see, but my fifteen-year old vow had been broken.
Thinking and writing as if my origins could only be
Euro-American had to go and undid the sandal
Of where I came from. I also didn't know, literally
Or geographically, how the bottom of my cultural
Vision fell out in the trip from Israel down to Cairo.
Most of all I didn't know that now I walked in Africa,
Or if I did it was less than feeling like the easy prey
Of hieroglyphic Egyptian gods like Horus the falcon,
Laughing Anubis, Ptah, the maker in the style of Thoth,
And in the ink of Seshat that milk of Isis washed away
If I was ever to meet Osiris and confess, "I live."

When I returned to my cabin in the forest near the monks
And to routine daily Mass, the unexpected Jericho
Vision and Egypt's disorienting me seemed to heighten,
Unlike when I was there, the religious experiences
That I remembered in Sinai and the rest of Israel.
Writing about them I had a new persona, Orpheus,
Put back together to sing of a reborn Eurydice.
Working through that, next I wanted to go back to Africa.
This time to witness and write new poetry about finding
How Catholic rituals and the saints resembled African
Ancestor worship and the traditions of animism.
Needless to add, perhaps, that idea was quickly blown away.
What I expected fell prey to the experience and died:

Festivals held in the Woodstock summer, 1969;
College becoming a counter culture, revolution ride;
Living and breathing high Western culture's promise to
        provide;
Finding the great code of art and God embodied in His bride;
Personal tragedy and how to recover deep inside.
What I expected from them compared to what really happened
Couldn't abide, but I see them fit to kneel and unstrap my
Sandal for something and someone coming, more powerful
        than I.
One sandal after another unstrapped for one more sandal on.
I see a sandal of many sandals, the Woodstock sandal.

Spring Fever, 1969, left to right: Harry Filkin, Kip Conner, Jim Jacobus, Charles Cantalupo,
John Lewis.

Between Shores

In the same moment as if immortal, hopelessly mortal;
Passion so totally self-possessing, always unchanging;
At the same time to combust or mutate suddenly, then gone;
Like a beginning before beginning, all polarizing;
And the desire come before desire can't be redemptive?

This I remember. No going back? To where and what? To
    whom?
Present as ever, this moment lets me step outside myself?
This is the bar down the shore in Jersey. Harry and Kip play
"Build Me Up Buttercup," "My Back Pages," "Walk Away
    Renee,"
"Gloria," "Honky Tonk Woman," "Mustang Sally," the Beatles,

"Happy Together," some Motown, don't forget "Mony,
    Mony."
Listening still, are they sixteen? Sixty? Seventy? Unchanged,
Standing with me I see Robin, Kenny, Peggy, and Judy,
Richard, and Bruce, and they're dancing, and I'm playing the
    same songs?
In the same moment as if immortal, hopelessly mortal;

Passion so totally self-possessing, always unchanging;
At the same time to combust or mutate suddenly, then gone.

Silence on either side of its being then or now, that shore….
How could I not turn around when I saw my house burning
    down
Just before sunrise?   And how could I not follow the sunset

Seeing the stars in the western sky above another shore
Never before either inside or outside my mind but where
It could all die neither more nor less than bedrock and ocean
I was beginning to hear, though not at first, but ever more
Clearly, except in the presence and the silence of redwoods.

Talk about being like gods, immortal, hopelessly mortal,
Passion so totally self-possessing, as if they know and
Even could dance good and evil?   How could I not want to see
More of this other shore? Getting back to my native land or
Making a new one on foreign soil? That's not the question.

Knowing the former and not knowing the latter? Not at all.
I'd rather be somewhere in between: between the violin
And a raw redwood slab lost in the Pacific and purple;
Somewhere between non-adventure and adventure, living with
Someone I love who loves me and blending into each other

Sometimes like shocking pink amaryllis all along the sea,
Other times camouflaged like the deer in grass during a
    drought;
Sometimes enclosing like eucalyptus trees over the road;
Other times like birds above, below and at my eye level;
Sometimes like sea urchins shining in the tidal crevasses.

Other times still shining like an amber glass lighthouse beacon.
Somewhere between shores – I start on one and move to
    another.
Who is that beautiful person riding down that glassy wave?

Or are those huge bodies lounging on the rocks at mid tide
    seals?
Two bites from either would rip my throat out, yet on a third
    shore.

Spring Fever reunion, 2019, left to right: John Lewis, Kip Conner, Charles Cantalupo, Jim Jacobus, Harry Filkin.

Return to Paris

"Africa…no Eritrea…I mean Europe" – a false start
After two Burgundies when I first try saying what this trip
Means to me forty years after my original visit:
Rue de Nesle's Day-Glo maroon and chartreuse room that I
        shared with…
Can't I remember the name or face? Not really but other
Details like siding with North Vietnamese in a café,
Crepe salesmen mocking this US student wearing a beret,
Wanting to memorize every piece of art, and my swearing
I would come back again still stick, and I have, half a dozen
Visits before the one I'm about to tell, since it means as
Much as the first if not more, if that could ever be the case.

Cash machines, Starbucks, and endless cell phone cases for sale
        on
Rue de Nesle rather than shady guys whose jackets are lined
        with
Watches, where I'm easy prey for any unnatural blond,
Don't make a difference; nor do east or west on this journey,
Traveling to or from life, and whether rising or falling –
Death either way inch by inch, and its eternal, lone city
Swooshing its syllables round a curve and every corner.

If this trip really amounts to more than what I've known before

May be irrelevant, pointless, or impossible to say.
Still why not try – to a music like a small boat and ocean,
Raven and tomb, and a stairway into sunshine with organ;
Praying the church on the mountaintop contains the sacred
       heart,
Calling the loved ones I lost forever back to life again,
As I go down brick by human brick to finding the mud stream
At the beginning and flowing under who I am, my house,
Man who becomes his own cross despite unchanging and
       young deer
Sipping the river of life above, mosaic and gold sky.
Yet the inscription's black letters seem to jump when I focus.
Satis, enough, becomes *numquam satis*, never satisfied.
Squinting I see *satis quod sufficit*: you decide enough.

Figuring, practicing ways to deal with such a dilemma
Typifies what I've been thinking since first coming here till
       now:
Taking the picture of history taking pictures of history;
Drafting it word by word: lizard, putti, butterfly, bullet,
Grapes in the baskets, and barrels; finding heralds of faces
Mourning, rejoicing, or simply being where none were before:
Lost in the folds of air, bodies, ecstasy, and flakes of gold;
Banishing foreign when I feel foreign; hearing the seashells
Lining the columns; committing more than merely complying
To the behaviors expected and the masks of protection
Only reserved for the dead and not the live and true profile
Faraway but no less certain close up; molding an altar
Out of indefinite; multiplying eyes in the locks or
Doorways' asymmetry painted more for volume not surface;
Hammering nail after nail as testimony of force and
Confidence: *trivium* nailed to the *quadrivium* with what
Have you to spur more than thinking this is just another trip.

Yet I return without wearing any medals of any
Power: an unconscious choice, but back then I didn't wear one.
What is the difference if nonbelievers block the rose window,
Bus stops and various masterpieces same as believers?
Back in the 70s Asian tourists took pictures of me
As I received in the furthest chapel east in Notre Dame
Holy Communion – but status as a specimen passed, too.
Seeing the same place roped off and stripped of kneelers and
     candles
This time around I refuse to kiss the relic of Christ's thorns'
Casing of silver, the *Agnus Dei* singing *peccata*
[M]*undi* and *vicit…sequamur* deep in my heart, regardless.
Otherwise how I could still be breathing when countless others
Who walked this city along with me *un étranger* are not?

Still I can see them and me there, too, expulsed from the
     garden,
And I'm re-entering graveyard portals, rickety gates, and
Weedy walls near lonely steeples waiting someone's death to
     toll.
Look! Uninhabited Alpine glaciers and promontories,
Birds of prey lacing the clouds with no horizon extending
Over a silent abyss except for echoes of *"La mort.*
C'est moi!" while crosses and graves wind through a dark
     mountain forest –
Passing through ruins made darker by what I can imagine
Haunts them because I recall them bright and wholly inspiring,
Making me confident: stately palms and eucalyptus shade
Planted by I don't know whom; a headless woman who poses,
Framed by an archway; the glowing martyr peacefully draped
     on
Torture that gives him his name and leads to I-don't-care power
Wreaking whatever wherever; blinding cypresses on fire,

Doves ripping open their meaty breasts and flying on their
    backs
Under a blue sun that wakens abstract blooms in a grotto
While a bat picks at the heart of two-faced romance cast in
    stone.
I can remember our being there together as artists,
Taking the photographs' photographs as portraits of spirits;
Writing graffiti – how vampire leaders can't ejaculate –
Watching a flaying conducted like a sacred violin
Constantly playing for eyes too gleaming through the heavy
    smoke –
Blood filling buckets, the victim hanging upside down, and us
Acting like innocent children, only satyr-taught to sing.

Tell me I didn't see this when I came previous visits?
It was more like noisy traffic speeding both sides of the Seine?
Or the department store La Samaritaine – not bankrupt then?
Maybe the roommate whom I forget could tell the real story?
Why no one's finger indented any marble and why no
Swan and a woman would lead to but hide total violence?
Crucifix and chandelier of human skulls can't have happened?
Shops and apartments on any street can't change into guitars,
Cellos, and orchestras? Can't I find a balcony window,
Cobblestone street, and a spiral staircase, however endless,
Back near where I was before no matter how many years pass?
Fountain of books and a stag's head? What's that obelisk-
    wearing
Elephant? Concave facades or nothing? This Aphrodite
Could be my daughter enfolded by my two other daughters
Out of the water, and all these others…are they still here, too?
Arrows of beauty from nowhere but the daily and always
Playing *Ars Nova* as if it never stops as it changes?

Still I can see them and me there, too: the preaching to fishes;
Someone else pursing his lips and taking off a big jacket,
Maybe his father's, before a fight with no chance of winning,
Which is won anyway. Let me be like him, I remember,
Thinking and seeing him later as he carried his father
And their gods not knowing where except for faith that they
     had them.
Others appear now: the one who wouldn't listen to my
     sssshhhh.
First the dogs spotted him. Later guards would feed him to the
     dogs.
Who was that woman whose hair looked like her only shirt, or
     was
That what I wanted to see? Her friend, his vascular arms of
Style and devotion, that rock of writing always in his hand?
Others – the one who would only bleed a drop from a deep cut.
Demeters, snakes, and Athenas. Gauls committing suicide?
Fruit in the arms of a young man made him half god, half
     woman.
I didn't know it all balanced on a tomb that was open
Where I was sitting: that wrapped up body, mother who
     claimed it,
Heavier second by second and collapsing all the arms
Bearing it up along with her, flowing all miraculous
Purple to darker deep waters, and beneath them another
Man who is lifting, his tendons straining and his hair flying.

Maybe another scene like what happened now instead of then
Also illuminates what I understand in returning.
One day while walking I pass a demonstration of chanting
Outside the Gare du Nord metro, "No! No Gbagbo and No
     Peace!"
Just before that in a church I found a lamp from a light bulb

Turned upside down, hollowed out, and filled with lamp oil
    and a wick.
Years ago I found the same thing in Malawi and sang, "Light!"
So much light and also darkness…am I some kind of magus
In a new forest of Paris, looking for the newborn, Silvia?

Rue Au Maire, Paris, December 1970, photo by Dave Glass, courtesy of Dave Glass.

Edgar Allan Poe in Richmond

Cary Street, 3 a.m., what's that clacking, ratchet in 4/4?
Blues riffs on washboard or *guiro, pua, rapido,* and drunks
Laughing like crazy below our window, each one's grinding tune
Waking me over and over? "I heard nothing and slept well....
Only a dream," you say next day when I tell you at breakfast.
Clickerty, clackerty, click clack, clack click, clackerty click rack....
Only a dream?   It feels real as now, today, and yesterday's

Glittering water's determined trickle into old brick and
Cobble stone streets where a black man still takes care of the ashes
Somewhere between Richmond's tallest building – brutish, erected
Over a parking garage, facing 95 – and some floor boards
Two hundred sixty years old or going one hundred fifty
More back to Powhatan, who's named Wahunsenacawh at birth,
And Pocahontas: the chief, his daughter; dealing with John Smith
And the first colonists to the point of marrying John Rolfe?
Better the British and Christianity weren't invented?

Who has done nothing to feel ashamed? The little bright
     islands,
Tree clumps, and rocks in the James? Why not let there be
     Rome again,
Built on these hills and a temple not mere brick but
     marble-faced –
First in the new world and fitting a republic to thrive at
Home in the liberty of its own words: buried exactly
Where they are written and spoken; rooted in the same ground;
     at
Home in the markets: tobacco, iron, cotton, grain, and slaves?
Also at home in the *clack crack, click crick, clankerty* drunks'
     song?

Or is that too much a letdown? Crazy dream within a dream
Vying with history? In between and hopelessly small scale
If not invisible, yet like sunlight playing in the leaves
If we look up in the trees, is that not Mordecai leaving
Synagogue? Samuel, tell me. VA DMV seems to
Dominate everything. Can I really see you and dirt streets,
Three-story houses the highest, mostly two and not the brick
Still to be found up and down these hills but wooden without
     paint?
No more than drunks grinding crazy music, in my dreams or
     not;
No more than ten thousand others of your fellow Richmondites;
Freed men and Indians; all the way down to the many more
Thousands of slaves to and from their market next to their
     graveyard
(Talk about lost in the *clank clank, rack clack, crackerty*) down
     from
Where we are sleeping on Cary: Shockoe Bottom, not quite the
Flowering gardens behind most of those old Richmond houses.
"Bottom" I get but the "Shockoe"? "Shockoe"? Saying it I peer

Into a church like a little Pantheon but plain and gray:
Couple of columns and funeral embellishments of urns,
Wrought iron spikes, and half open shells but really a mass
    tomb,
So says the plaque on it, where a local blue blood packed
    theater
Burns down the night after Christmas, when my reason to be
    here
Almost aged two could have burned up with them: or should I
    say "burned"
Once and for all since he burned before and after not only
Up and down Shockoe and any other places that claimed him,
He barely wanting or able to claim any; Virginia,
Nevertheless, making the best case for his being its…son?
That's what I'm seeing in Richmond? Maybe, yet not forgetting
"Want of parental affection" is, in his words, his worst pain.
Two weeks before Richmond's aristocracy incinerates,
Poe's mother dies of tuberculosis: she who, in his words,
"Looks with contempt on the mediocrity…of a king," or
Poe does at least in comparing her work as an actor who
Consecrates herself to beauty; thus does he "from child-hood's
    hour…
Not see… / [a]s others" see "in" his "childhood," barely
    aware of
Anything but his new middle name or brand of pain: "Allan."

Out of or into the fire, it burns but not so directly
Into his flesh and more slowly, cooler: colder with more death,
Seemingly warm at first with a word; the *clackerty crack crick*
Spelling the syllables of "established" as if they could be
Anything more than some scintillations in a long poem –
Something that doesn't exist; a simple, flat contradiction.
Orphan of actors and brought to worship right where the
    theater

Burns itself into a tomb called Monumental Church; *"finis"* –
History shouts at the actors – *clank clack, clinkerty* be damned?
Not that things looked quite as bad at first: the delicate oval
Portraits gold framed and the state star woven into the bedding;
Endless white violets, lovers' seats, and classical verse at
Ease in the orris root air with pillars, porticoed temples,
Whether in church or at home, and clear views down to the
     river,
Surging with "Come to me," power, and, "Jump in. Swim,
     swim, swim, swim…."
Who would have thought every dollar, book, and comfort
     would be lost,
Coming back home, and the slaves not even caring who he was,
Playing their *clickerty, click clack* – master boy nothing to them;
Iron, tobacco, and cotton with their flesh going to market?

Not the whole story but scintillations, that word again, and
Not merely bio but what the place, in this case it's Richmond,
More or less randomly adds to make this kind of pilgrimage
Minor heroic in form, with one more way to find the Poe:
Clickerty, clank click, "a dream within a dream," you said to me.
Was it facetiously even though I claimed the dream was real?
Somehow the words, if they're words, the "*Clack, clink, clickerty,*
     clank, crank"
Intimate something about Poe here, not only rational,
Scattered all over the surface, deeper, deeper, and deeper;
Some kind of music I never would have followed until now:
Driving itself into what I say and *the* way to say it;
Structure subverted by losing where it thinks it should follow,
Conscious designs notwithstanding, so that spontaneity
Dominates thinking and tone however paradoxically:
Clackenting ratchets in drunken 4/4, breaking the same way;
Dactyls and trochees to match the sub- or unconscious
     demands –

Making it or should I say returning to the oral first,
If unexpectedly, real and / or imagined, or in dreams,
Conjuring metrically with remains of place and the poet?

Thus, I see Poe reappear, aged twenty-six, establishing
Manly and writer's credentials – if such words may be allowed;
"Poe" and "establishing" still an oxymoron, at least in
His time though nevermore now. A term like "normalcy" also
Could be applied to his coming back to Richmond and making
Writing itself the most sane and steady, rational, constant
Part of his being despite the horror stories more famous
Both in his art and his life; his writing; melody, meter,
Narrative, character, image, language, and intelligence:
Even his penmanship – perfect!   The best place he'd never
     leave:
Found when he moves back to Richmond, in the summer when
     it's hot,
And that he keeps, thank God, even though he leaves by
     twenty-eight,
Till the penultimate moments of his life, when he comes back,
Twelve years elapsed and all written out but welcomed once
     again.

"[All] is right….I have success," Poe writes in 1836.
Good health and money, Canova-looking wife, the Capitol
Never too far out of sight, his "reputation…extending,"
Richmond "friends…open arms" – bring on Roman legions
     surrounded,
Marching through walls of flames to the gates of hell.   Why not
     feel this,
Being the editor of a great new journal and knowing
He has a vision of southern writing culture to match his
New England rivals and all their self-important novelties?
Make way: the SLM, *Southern Literary Messenger* –

"Literature...Every Department...and...Fine Arts" its devotion.
All the years of his transcribing lines from Shakespeare and
     Milton,
Classical prosody, and his hard work come to fruition.
Why not tell poets they stink worse than their paper, and they
     should
Grab a gun if there's a chance to end their misery? Why not
Walk with the gorgeous Virginia Clemm up Shockoe Hill streets
     and
See Allan dead in his grave? And then go back to editing:
All for himself but for other writers, too; countless letters –
Raising the SLM's circulation high as anyone's,
British included; the manuscripts and money rolling in....
Why not a story? It scintillates – its *clankerty crank grank*:
Someone reports in a recent *Christian Sentinel* how he
Helped a drunk get off the street. He reaches into his pocket,
Opens a box and says, "Take one. My dead beautiful wife's
     teeth."
Mordecai's version is: Poe went walking near Shockoe market,

Richmond (1817) drawn by Charles Fraser (1782-1860) and engraved by John Hill (1770-1850), courtesy of the Edgar Allan Poe Museum, Richmond, Virginia.

Where a slave rattles a gourd to which more slaves sing, "*click,*
    clack, click."
Poe asks the master, "What's that?" He's drunk and laughs,
    "It's your wife's teeth."
Mabbott and nobody else reports on any other source.

Act three of Richmond in Poe, excuse me, that's "Poe in
    Richmond" –
Richmond not Allan would be a better middle name for him –
Opens with Poe writing, "It's no use to reason with me now."
He wants to go home to die: Virginia dead and *Eureka*
"Done," he says. He can "accomplish nothing more" than feel
    "depressed."
That's on July 19, '49 but forty days later
He could sing, can "It…be" me "on / whom thy tempests fell all
    night?"
"Nothing but praise" from the papers, rave reviews, and
    gratitude
For the "nativity" of the boy from Richmond now famous –
All for his writing. He's even known in France, the …*Whig*…
    reports.
"Nothing but kindness," distinguished invitations, and love is
Paving the way to his being absolutely established.
"After so many deaths, I live…write…. / And relish versing.
    Oh,
[M]y only light…." Can he really be imagined singing this?
Clickerty, clackerty, click clack, clack click, clackerty click rack….
Forty days later he's dead, found derelict in Baltimore.
Classical tragedy? After all, he's recognized as great.
Or is it tabloid? "The papers here are praising me to death."
In his last letter to Clemm, Poe writes this without irony.

What does this place seem to answer? Nowhere can evoke him
    more:

Come out of iron and slaves; tobacco-fed to be pounded
Into fine grain; to be spun like cotton down the mighty James;
Classical columns provide the frame and stage for re-entrance.
Enter he does and more totally abstracted than ever,
Says his best translator, Baudelaire; yet like the tallest pine
Blasted by lightning and wind, to topple powerlessly on
Monte altissimo, where it grows (see Horace, *Odes* 2.10).
Long little scrolls of the works he wants to read fill his pockets.
Raven black clothes melt to dove white in the Richmond
        summer heat.
Mothers and children run out to greet him walking Richmond's
        streets.
Lectures unfold like an orris root perfume: "The Poetic
Principle" out to "The Raven" – unforgettable, "graceful,"
"Musical," "full of strong sense," and "clear" – the voice one
        gorgeous flow.
He sees Elmira, his lost love, sitting now in the front row.
Later he's climbing the hill up to her home and meets backers
For his new journal, the highest glory, christened the *Stylus,*
Jesus to SLM's John….   Now see him lecturing the crowd
Gathered in wonder at the esteemed Exchange Hotel. See him
Reading to friends out at Talavera's farm, the first yellows
Tingeing September's full leaves; and that idyllic Norfolk scene:
Moonlight and ocean and Poe on the veranda reciting
"Annabel Lee" and "The Raven," with an "Ulalume" encore.
Pretty young women in formal gowns surrounding him love it.

Who can say what goes wrong? No pretending. Spare the
        simplistic.
Drinking or temperance? Mother, father – gone? Eurydice
Lost as *Eureka*? The scintillations versus established?
Grankety, clackerty, imp of the perverse? *Clink, grack, clack, crack*?

Plenty of details here complicate a much better story:
Far more than I can provide, including ugly skyscrapers,

DMVs, who empties ashes out of what. Still here's a few:
Views of the river now blocked by corporate offices and cars;
Columns and portico where the boy grew up now disappeared;
Even the building replacing it condemned, and graffiti:
"Ion. Fuck cops" on the peeling turquoise bricks once rich
        brown red
Still making much of the downtown, older buildings so pretty.
SLM offices?   Same fate, but the bricks are painted white.
Grave of Elmira? It's fetishized with smooth James River
        stones.
Maybe I've fetishized Poe in Richmond much in the same way?
Visiting Hollywood Cemetery, where he used to play:
Cliffs overlooking the river, in his day called Harvey's Woods,
Jefferson Davis's tomb all dignified just up the way.
What can I say of the blood-stained banners, thousands and
        thousands
Buried there, haunting today?   They might just as well have
        been slaves?

Or should I run away, taking refuge, like Richard Crashaw
Making Loreto's Shrine of Our Lady home in his old age,
Only the shrine is to Poe and filled with all kinds of relics,
Many of which I note in this poem – yet so many more:
SLM building beams; bricks from Greenwich Village where he
        lived
Almost as famously as he did in Richmond at the end;
Gentle black cat to make school girls scream if they read the
        story;
Quinn's bust of Poe or at least a copy with lipstick kisses.
Poe priest Chris Semtner is the best one to tell all the rest.
Listen to him and the *clank grank, grock clink, clackerty clack
        click….*

At the Grave of Hilda Doolittle (H.D.)

I say "Greek flower" if that means I live one hundred yards
    north
Of H.D.'s grave and "Greek ecstasy / reclaim[s]" her through
    the great
Epitaph she wrote herself that's written on a flat grey stone –
Nine other Doolittle flat stones near her: 1844-
2007; with Hilda, 1886 to when,
Aged ten, I marveled that 1961 still looked the same
If it was turned upside down, which I remember here because
Language had nothing else better than this strangeness back
    then, and
All of my children by ten or even younger have come with
Me to this grave on our countless walks since this cemetery
Borders our neighborhood on the south and, known as Nisky
    Hill,

Overlooks archaeologic-like black quieted steel mills
Of equal altitude, and the Lehigh River in between.

Saying "Greek flower" here might seem as strange as the upside
      down
Numbers still reading the same – or even stranger amidst oaks,
Sycamores, maples, catalpas, gingkoes, willows, and lindens
Dwarfing the ruined Victorian and neoclassical
Obelisks, crosses, and mausoleums. Saying "Greek flower"?

Say it, I do, and it grounds me here instead of the blast of
"[E]cstasy," outside where I live, I love, I believe in one…
"Lamb who has conquered" and "*agnus noster…eum sequamur.*"

Following? What? When I also say the words on her brother's
Stone next to hers? "Fell in action…1918…in France" at
"Thiacourt…laid to rest," thirty-three, machine-gunned, St.
      Mihiel?

No words at all to say on the stones of two infants dead in
Less than six months that her father's first wife had before she
      died,
Age twenty-one, who is buried there with H.D's parents, aunt,
Sister, and brother who lived, a niece, too – all of them only
ID'd with names and their dates, unlike their Hilda and Gilbert.
Not that no epitaph makes them any less significant.

I say "Greek flower" precisely for this reason above all –
Their names and dates mean the traumas war and poetry have
      missed:
"[M]ute" and "inglorious," as a poem stamps it, and all the
Triumphs of life over art, which no one knows or can number
Fully enough without falling and succumbing the same way.

Hilda Doolittle, 2 years and 8 months; Harold Doolittle, 1 year and 7 months; Gilbert Doolittle, 4 years and 7 months, Eggert Studio, Bethlehem, PA, courtesy of H. D. Papers, American Literature Collection, Beinecke Rare Book and Manuscript Library, Yale University.

47 | At the Grave of Hilda Doolittle (H.D.)

I say "Greek flower" and live in the same neighborhood of…
     what?
Historic Bethlehem? Meaning architecture is preserved,
Fake old or really old long lost as a factor, the ancient
Trees not preserved but chopped down for shrubs or impassive
     hybrids;
Doolittle's house knocked down for a city hall to be put up
Brutalist style meaning murder all the poetic beauty.

Then I walk out the front door at 442 High Street where we
Live, and eventually I walk to the graveyard and the grave,
More times than not, but it's hard to find exactly when I look.
I know the general area, but all the same flat stones:
"Which one is hers," I've said, many times alone but pretending
Not to be lost when I show her grave to family and friends
Who've never seen it. Late winter snowdrops first bloom there.
     How's that
For a cliché of a poet's grave? In winter a good snow
Buries the stone, and the graveyard walk is too slippery with
     ice.

Scallop shells threaded with ribbons crown the lintel of our
     house –
Somewhat Victorian, brick and built in 1895.
Might she have seen them? No other house has such
     decoration.
Furthermore, seashells, when it's not winter, help me find her
     grave:
Nautilus, scallops, and snails – the common, strange, or
     whatever –
Visitors leave on the stone, which make it different from the
Other flat stones set around it. But why shells? As in "Sea
     Rose,"

"Rose, harsh rose / marred and with stint of petals / …you…
    caught in the drift…. /
[F]lung on the sand, / you are lifted /…in the wind," but not
    until
She calls it, "more precious / than a wet rose / single on a stem"?
Or could the shells invoke "Helen"? – "All Greece hates / the
    still eyes" and
"All Greece reviles / the wan face when she smiles…. / Greece
    sees… / God's daughter
 [B]orn of love /…if she were laid… / amid funereal cypress"?
"Greece" as in *Iliad*; "sea," "Sea Rose" – together leading to
"So you may say" – on the epitaph – "Greek flower," and
    joining
H.D.'s "Greek ecstasy" that she says "reclaims" her "forever"?

What is *re*claims" and "forever"? No one really can know.
    What?
Other than some kind of blankness? "[A]gnus…eum sequamur"?
Or a conclusion predictably absurd and destructive?

"Lovefeast," Moravians call it, with a sugary cookie.
H.D. herself wrote a little on Moravian mystics.
Some of her readers are liberated if she's an icon:
Feminist, Freudian, *Imagiste*, bisexual – something
Other than "ecstasy," that is, death "forever," nothing more.

I say "Greek flower" instead, although "America," "Rome," or
"Africa" works just as well to get away from that certain
"[E]cstasy," echoed in "fell in action," written for Gilbert.
"[F]ollowing / intricate song's lost measure" is what comes after
"[R]eclaims forever." So she "died," she says; her cause of
    death was;
She "fell in action," and she devoted her work to only

"[F]ollowing intricate song's lost measure." Following.
     Measure.
Intricate. Song. But why lost? Lost? Is it? I say "Greek
     flower."
Say this with me at the grave of H.D. "Flower. Greek flower."

Gateway

At a beginning I saw both death and life in the gateway.
Death didn't stay, so I went through, but now I've come back
    again.
Seeing death has come back, too, I don't know if life ever left.

What if the gateway reveals itself more than either of them?
What if the universe wants it not only to live or die,
One pillar newly restored, the other left original?

What if the green in the gateway moves through every color
Into a black and white nowhere near as still but shimmering
Always as much more than any expectations first or less?

What is that mantra? That "pass me by, pass me by" whistling
Like my new mantra the gateway keeps on singing to the world
On one condition. The world would come back – no way it
    could not.

Don't ask me how; ask the gateway. Go by its vision not mine:
As in a folktale-like sailor's grave found deep in lonely
    woods....
"Pass me by, pass me by," I hear, walking to the rocky shore.

What if no foothold there joins the gateway's ocean of language
To the horizon until there's no horizon anymore?
One sheet of sky and sea? Nothing to distinguish but twelve
    notes

Out of invisible waves in fog the gateway beckons through?
Faintly fluorescent, a signature of "work" etched on its arch?
What other gifts of God could I ask for more than to be asked?

Thinking performance and force, who's not wiped out at the
    gateway?
Who doesn't die in the storm without the notes within the
    notes,
Words within words, and the rhythms in the rhythms'
    person of

Person? How else not to stay and keep on loving the gateway?
Loving the music between the knowing and the unknowing?
Each time a word appears for the music. Listen. It changes,

Changes, and changes. The words line up and fall. Each
    time a
Story appears for the music, hear it change and change again.
Every story lines up and falls. Each time a rhythm plays –

Is it too short or too long? – the music changes and changes.
Every rhythm lines and up falls. Each time a meaning drifts
Out of the music, it changes, making every meaning

Line up and fall. Yet each time an expectation arises
Out of the music; it changes. Each expectation merely
Lines up and falls. Or if hope for something stirs with the
    music,

How could it not change when it has changed so many times
     before?
Hopes line up also and fall.   What couldn't be broken pieces
Come to the gateway? I come here, too, maybe only dreaming

How they work all at once. Stop, then work again. Stop. Work
     and start
Falling and falling and falling, and I'm nothing but silent.
Only the joy and the silliness of it – with some waltz, too –

Might let me speak of it later, when I'm marching and
     marching,
One foot in front of the other but in my mind always
     somewhere
Falling and falling, not thinking of the end but of that gateway.

Eritrea, 2002, photo by Lawrence F. Sykes, courtesy of Lawrence F. Sykes.

Domicile

Grandeur in any of its moods, but especially in that of
extent, startles, excites – and then fatigues, depresses. For
the occasional scene nothing can be better – for the constant
view nothing worse.

> Edgar Allan Poe, "The Domain of Arnheim"

Night of the first freeze and I rush out to cover annuals –
Coleus, elephant ears, impatiens, other things I bought
Over the summer, but now I can't remember what they're
    called:
No more exotic than *Strobilanthes* and *Draceana,*
Persian Shields, Green Spikes, and *Hypoestes* all polka dotted.
Grabbing the bed sheets and tablecloths too raggedy or stained
Out of the back of the linen closet, dining room hutch, and
Pile in the basement of drop cloths, I still don't have enough to
Cover as many plants as I want to, letting three ferns too
Pot-bound and old to live – *Bostoniensis* – six more months
    inside,
Hang from the Japanese maple, so that showers of blood red
Leaves intertwine with the dying fronds as sacrifice made to
What I'm not sure, but it feels like some acknowledgement that I

Fail in my efforts to save from death the life in this garden,
Likewise in everything else, but I can try, as I do with
Covering plants as a kind of rite and one of many more
I get obsessed with in autumn: "rite" or seasonal chores, too,
Yet maybe more like a pathological virginity,
Like Proserpina deluded, thinking dragged into darkness
Might be escaped picking flowers; maybe more like a conflict:
One voice and silence or countless uncontrolled and breaking
        more
Into the meaningless than a meaning ever could handle?
What kind of chores can embody such abstractions and get
        done,
As if like some kind of sacred duty perfectly mundane –
OCD, I will admit it, somewhat, still feeling worthwhile
Like a domestic or minor kind of soul-feeding beauty?

Three or four weeks ago, seasonal denial first hit me.
Thinking about all the plants that must come in or they would
        die,
Also how heavy they'd be to carry, plus all the big mess
Outside and in, I felt dread but more so like doing nothing:
Grabbing the Nashe with his "Farewell… / Summer bids you
        farewell…
Archers and bowlers" – and "surfers," I say – meet
        "/ desolation… /
Silence… / …slow marching…descend I to the fiends" and "
        [w]eep heavens,
[M]ourn earth" and "here Summer ends," still singing, "Borne
        on the bier with" –
Uh-oh that's Shakespeare's line – "satyrs…wood nymphs,"
        Nashe and me, at least.

Anyway, washing the windows comes before plants move
        inside,

Aztec God of corn, 2020, photo by Barbara Cantalupo, courtesy of Barbara Cantalupo.

57 | Domicile

Craving their light the way we do while we love to look
        through them.
Therefore, why not once a year with Windex – wiping the grime
        off,
Losing some sanity hanging out the second and third floors.
Glass in the windows of our late nineteenth-century house has
Ripples where clarity comes back like a poem in detail –
Shot through, entangled, to serve no purpose, alien or shared
Other than seeing as if I had not ever seen before
What I'm not sure of, again, beyond the total unstitching
Up to the sky that unstitches, too, if I see it or not,
On either side of the window, clean or blurrier than hell.
Still I know no job so satisfying when I see it done
Other than…stop me from going back to unified, sealed off
Poetry, monologues when there's so much more to do outside.

Take my *jardin Africain.* No way my Bethlehem PA,
Winter, Moravian, Christmas city, once a proud steel town
Now a casino called "Sands" would tolerate such a bower,
Real and imagined if I don't break down, box, and put away
Everything but the base of the fountain, stone grapes, stone
        garlands
Draping motifs of stone skulls reflected in the stone mirror
Held by the statue of "Sight" not only allegorically
Holding the northernmost garden spot and pretty as a child.
Otherwise bye-bye to basins full of water and their pump,
Hand brooms from Casamance, plastic trumpets, old
        calabashes,
Strings of bamboo lights with beads and bells entwining lobster
        boat
Ropes hung in two-story yews enclosing heavy green chairs
        that
Also get dragged to the cellar, after they're scrubbed and hosed
        down,

Leaving the patio's ancient flagstones fending for themselves.
Rites of removal extend to long dead, anatomic, and
Twisted wisteria limbs our neighbors prune, which I scavenge,
Setting up sculptures with Maasai beads around a big table.
Next come the sections of broken snake arranged among
        flowers –
Yucatán spotted ceramic stretched out, camouflaged in soil.
Elsewhere I gather the pieces of a Moroccan platter,
Under a bush by the side door in a circle, and some shoes
Also left out in the garden for the summer: Brazilian
Yellow high heels bought on impulse, which nobody ever wore,
Rotting for years but still beautiful; and one pair of *shida*,
Hard rubber sandals from Eritrea, worn by its fighters
During their thirty-year revolution for independence;
My little monument lost in ferns but like the oversized
Pair in the roundabout in Asmara that's called *Shida* Square.
Under the weeping and fading willow, easily unseen,
Last is a statue from Cameroon – red clay, foot high, hollow,
Set on an altar of stray bricks I dug out of the garden
Decades ago and washed clean now by the weather ever since.
No St. Fiacre, quaint shovel in the ground and simpering
Who needs a woman – it is a woman. I used to rattle
Seeds in her body before her neck broke. Her left leg broke, too.
Why they were sealed in her I don't know, but somehow, I lost
        them.
I didn't want to put more in when I glued her pieces back.
Anyway what kind of seeds? – her looks seemed powerful
        enough,
Not needing anything else from me: her rippling coiffure and
Hemisphere eyebrows all bullet-pocked and begging holy
        beads;
Face like good bread for the hungry; straight-ahead eyes and
        big teeth

Beckoning through her full lips while she pulls big long breasts
        and stands
Strong and presiding; impervious but not I-don't-know-you
Attitude, leaving some room for unintended, multiple
Interpretations and just as much for single-minded tropes
Aimed her way, resting on weathered bricks beneath forsythia,
And when I move her inside, the last thing after all the plants.

Lugging them in takes all day and so does lugging them
        outside
Seven months later in spring. The Norfolk pine has grown too
        tall,
Scraping the extra high ceiling on the second-floor landing.
So does the parlor palm overwhelm our dining room's lofty
Heights and black walls graced with herons. Plants? I should
        be saying trees –
Them versus me or too big and heavy? Feels like a who-dies-
First kind of question if I don't simply give them away or
Leave them outside if I want to some year. Am I at that point?
It's a refrain, a pre-dirge that plays in all my limbs up and
Down the stairs carrying fifty more plants, succulents, cacti….
But when I turn around for no reason, look at them arranged
Hanging in windows, against the walls, on tables, in corners,
Some in new places and others back like old friends who won't
        die,
What can I feel but some satisfaction, seeing some beauty
Saved, unavoidable doom put off a few seasons longer.
Then I remember – the vacuum going, cleaning up the dirt
Tracked in with bugs and debris predictably – still to come in,
Propped temporarily out of sight beneath the dogwood tree –
That little statue from Cameroon can't be left outside. No.
Nevertheless, I'm unsure in which plant it will not fall over.

Seasonal chores that feel like some ancient rite or compulsion

Haunt me when spring unfolds, too, as Hardy asking the
      question –
"How do you know, crocus root? / How do you know?" – in a
      poem
Published when World War I started, 1914. So am I,
Twenty-first century bourgeois and technology addict
Further away from permission or too lost and remote in
History serving another day's agenda to wonder
Helplessly much the same way if only for a little while?

Questions and feelings like this propel me one job to the next –
Rarely confessing to anyone they're there, not including
All the above and their minor, in part mock autumnal rite
Phenomenology. Therefore, getting firewood from Ben Scholl
Naturally follows as one more absolute. He owns the last
Farm stand and orchards remaining in our overbuilt city.
Ben dumps a cord of well-seasoned hardwood back in our
      alley,
After we talk about this year's apples: Honeycrisp, Melrose,
EverCrisp – being my favorites – all the cider he's making,
Farmers who sell him the wood, and how this year's been for
      growing.
I take my wheel barrow, fill it thirty times or so and roll,
Wobbling a lot and not sure if creaking means this year it
      breaks –
Back down the path to the open shed connected to our house.
Stacking the logs floor to ceiling on the southern wall, I smell
Some kind of ripening, fertile, solid warmth where I see wood
Cleanly and darkly block out the light through slats in the pink
      shed.
Gathering scraps for some kindling, hoping I can remember
Big green tomatoes and lavender hydrangea I should pick
When I have finished the wood, I laugh out loud at my
      thinking,

Last night when Ben called to tell me he would bring it this
     morning,
I should be starting to write this and not stuck with getting
     wood.
I mean that getting wood, washing windows, taking in the
     plants,
Breaking the African garden down are what makes the writing
Happen and not the reverse. Why else, all annuals gone or
Only a few frozen brown remaining, would massive flocks of
Ragged and rackety crows return like echoing caverns
Where a continuo of my raking, raking, and raking
Leaves and more leaves and more leaves plays out below and
     forms a pile
Higher and higher as dusk comes early, mask of unwanted
Cold on my face with lips open, dry yet tasting the red wine
I will drink later inside before I go back out in the dark?

On a Tree

Buzz saws and chippers accompany these lines to a maple,
"Seeldom," in Spenser's words, "inward sound," but all that
    remained of
Six large trees lately destroyed next door; the neighbor afraid
    that
This one would fall on him sleeping in his hammock, and
    leaves were
Dirty, and his wife and children didn't feel like getting crushed.
We shared the shade, but the maple grew on his side of the line,
Seven or eight feet, and fifteen years ago in late August
During a thunderstorm half the tree split, falling in our yard.

Nevertheless, the tree's other half remained and grew back
    strong.
I watched the wound get hard and the bark close over the split,
    but
Several dead branches and still the scar there panicked my
    neighbor,
Just the way previous neighbors next door also reacted –
Seeing a limb on the ground post-storm meant it tried to kill
    them.
Could something be in the water of that house making them
    think
Raising their property's value meant improving it, *sans* trees?

Now they're all gone and the house denuded. Happy and safe?
    Cursed.
That's what the place says to me in our historic and urban
District where, frankly, a lot of others chop down their massive
Trees without thinking except of sketch-thin, passive
    replacements
For this oasis of green that Google Earth pictures reveal
Lonely in otherwise unplanned asphalt, concrete, and ugly
Sprawl called the Valley and where I never would have lived
    unless
Old trees and just as old architecture offered assurance
As much as nature and forests all around my house before
Moving here – calling it home for us to raise our family.

Nikolaus Ludwig von Zinzendorf moved here in the eighteenth
Century – 1740s. Where's his tree and the bronze plaque
Saying he planted it? Overnight replaced with some red mulch.
Nine decades after Count Zinzendorf, did tree-loving Gustav
Grunewald know something I didn't when he painted his
    landscapes
Based on this area: broken stumps in every foreground,
Even when shade and exotic laurels parted for snaky
Trunks thick with river silt overhanging people placed like
    birds?

Hard hat with cigarette, belly, ass crack, wraparound mirror
Sunglasses, chain saw, and swagger, do you know what I'm
    saying?
Taking another step back, dear neighbors, you might think I
    sound
Like a believer in dryads, if that word can still be known:
Spirits who live within trees and die when they do, but that's
    not
Really what I want to say, or closest to that would be the

Lines from the psalm about wanting trees to hang our harps
     upon.

Actually that's what I called the maple half that remained when
It split before. Yet to fill the aching, empty space I chose
Five weeping willows or *Salix babylonica* for shade;
Hoping for then what I can see now: the shade beneath their
     sway;
Refugee squirrels and displaced birds recovering there with
Ivy below – that these neighbors also ruthlessly destroy,
Sacred to Bacchus or not; the shade of some presentiment,
Knowing our split maple's shade would not survive if our
     neighbors
Thought much about it, yet knowing willow shade would
     provide when
"Paramours" – Spenser again – like this lost maple disappeared;
Almost impervious shade despite the maple's being gone;
Shade and protection becalming: perfect first for recalling
This humble maple, however unsound inwardly, next for
Knowing this tree joins the other great trees, real or imagined,
Fallen or growing, beginning "in the midst of the garden":
Knowledge and life never ending. How could they ever mean
     less –

Towering pin oak outside my bedroom when I was a child
Up to my harping so sentimentally on this maple
And in between? I remember sprouting Jesse trees with
     Christs,
Davids, and more from their loins entwirling medieval
     windows,
Sculptures, and stories; the garden olives golden as my God's
Agony; olives that grow in deserts, waterless and strong;
Willows I planted and lost; the poplar trees and strange fruit,
     slaves;

Cedars with leopards and martial eagles; baobabs studding
Outstretched savannas aspiring to democracy; palm trees
Balancing entrances, streetlights, quays, and avenues with
        peace;
Redwood sequoias in love with moss enfolding their strong
        arms;
Sycorax trees full of voices breaking out of their prison
While eucalyptus trees count their silver. What of unlucky
Trees become stumps for the drunk to sit on, looking like
        stumps, too?
Or that bleached tree trunk I saw used as a gate among
        countless
Entrances leading to hell? And forests gnawed down for
        charcoal,
Long burned-out butts and burnt candles stuck in emerald
        mantels
Shredded by downpours like spikes. I see continuums of trees.

Then there's the tree I reported to my father as he died.
Only the wind blowing through it made me not hallucinate,
Driving in rain forest down a conch shell highway to a bay,
Black sand and turquoise, the beach all roots and rippling
        everywhere
From one big tree like a tree of trees consisting of banyans,
Baobabs, pines amid palms and olives, peaches and ginkgoes,
More I can't name, yet the branches bursting turpentine, mastic,
Ripe cloves, and rainbows of flowers, snakes, and bees in and
        out of
Burning or smoldering, maybe it was sprouting...who could
        tell?

One more tree comes to mind in the empty air once a maple:
Measureless sycamore near the rift where each of us comes
        from:

Granite and wood share its trunk while blossoms, buds, green
    leaves and dry
Go round continually with new fruit every season
As if the tree came before them and would be there when
    they're gone.
Under it orchestras play and banquets carry on and on.
Touching this tree recalls names and words I still can believe in.
Look up at noon and the sky shines through like stars that point
    a way
Out of the sadness and death this Norway maple reveals today.

Large old Sycamore *Ficus sycomorus* near Segeneyti, Eritrea, photo courtesy of Creative
Commons.

Africa Antetranslation

Bless thee…. Thou are translated.

William Shakespeare,
A Midsummer Night's Dream (3.1.105)

Open the curtain. Act II – I'm laid out in a tie-dye suit;
Minimal music and smoke machines in lurid light; wavy
Mylar like vertigo background; chorus trying to dance in
Colorful body bags. Center stage a vampy big woman,
Anima Animal, so I've named her – half soul and half beast –
Dressed like the "wild…gorgeous" girlfriend Joseph Conrad in
    Heart of
Darkness gives Kurtz when he's captured, and she challenges
    his world
Wordlessly since it can't know her language unlike her lover.
"I really think I would…shoot her," someone else in the story
Comments, suggesting the outcome if, regardless, she spoke
    out.
Meanwhile the play has her tower over me as if dead and
Offer her hand so I live again as if with her power.
Thinking I'm crazy to be performing poetry I wrote
After I visited Africa the summer before, when
My reputation depended on supposedly much more

Serious matters and not such spectacles, as I hold her
Hand and walk off as if into a new life, I don't care what
Anyone thinks of me, writing about Africa or not:
Not very scholarly, losing my religion, and acting
Like I'm on drugs, a professor soon to be out of a job.

Back to the woman in Conrad and her silence, reflecting
"Tenebrous…passionate soul," her "hush" becoming "the…
     whole land."
This is a moment before translation, which never happens.
See "Her eyes" gleam "back at us…the dusk…before she"
     disappears.
"She talked like…fury to Kurtz," but no one knows or speaks
     her tribe's
"[D]ialect" other than…Kurtz, of course – and she wields its
     power.
What does she say is the question. Who can translate except
     Kurtz?
Nobody else in the story. What prevents them and even
Silences Kurtz till his last breath of "The horror! The horror!"
Makes Conrad's story: its characters essentially doomed to
Missing what she has to say – or as I tried to stage at first –
Africa has to say. But my play was all my own words, too.
Anima Animal, my salvation, didn't speak a word.
How could I be unaware I duplicated this pattern?
I can't remember if I was asked or not, although someone
Criticized body bags on the chorus – hiding the actors'

Race when they were black and white, and I was obviously
     white.
Even now when I look back was race this play's biggest
     problem?
It was a moment before translation, which never happened,
Starting and stopping with nothing but what I wanted to say.

Logo of "Against All Odds: African Languages and Literatures into the 21st Century," Asmara, Eritrea, January 11-17, 2000," painting by Yegizaw Michael, courtesy of Yegizaw Michael.

What is the language of Conrad's "apparition," the "gorgeous…
[W]oman" who stands still and faces us but "slowly" walks
     away?
What would she say? And Kurtz translate? Make it beautiful
     as her.
Or should "formidable silence" and the issues Kurtz can raise
Keep us from hearing her voice and any other African's –
Or their translation, at least? – throughout the story as said by
Chinua Achebe way back in 1975? No,
I understand her in my imagination, hearing her
Make a world out of the language of her choice for whomever
Speaks it or translates. No other limits, purpose, agendas,
Or fundamentals can matter: alibiing winds of change,
Jesus or Allah, tradition, color, blackness or whiteness,
Marxists or entrepreneurs, decrees, diasporas, western,
Heritage, capital, human rights, Pan-Africa, Mother
Africa, strong man or woman, I T, globalization,
Ethnic, democracy, trade, exceptions, essences, the trans-
National, orient, ghosts, abstractions, altars, race, rainbows,
Guns, bread, and war – add whatever testimony you want,
     but…
Africa semper aliquid novi, something new always
Comes out of Africa. Is another renaissance to come

When what the African woman doesn't say in Conrad's story
Finally begins to be heard? Of course, it's not in my language.
But the words have their own spell or, less dramatically: listen
First and say nothing and listen, listen…something is in it
Faraway from any words I know yet taking me back to
Where they begin and then mixing in and…what? Is it joining,
Freeing them? Deepening, purifying them to be my own?
Origins different but still the feeling, I'm this person, too,
 And not a stranger? This land is not strange? Neither of us is

Dead? We connect through the words that lead us only
        together
Back to them or through the dread of being silenced before this?
Tell me that hieroglyph. Is it over five millennia?
Now hear me say it in your way true to mine and with love, too.
Something is missing? It's close…and like that sycamore, just
        as
Anciently singing four seasons all at the same time – lyrics
Translating into the names I hold most dearly and against
Fear that my loved ones are taken from me, yet as in a dream
I can't cry, whisper, or breathe? But even then, what is that
        stele:
Towering at the beginning, sun and quarter moon inscribed;
Trying to read it…the dust, or tears, or too much light in my
        eyes?

Ngũgĩ wa Thiong'o in Eritrea

"Farewell to English…for any of my writings. From now on
It is Gĩkũyũ and Kiswahili all the way," Ngũgĩ
Famously stated in 1986, and he became
African languages' greatest hero for literature,
Not knowing then "all the way" would lead him to Eritrean
Writing in African languages, in literature and
Orature, "all the way" back, millennia; continual,
Written examples, unceasing, and where the colonial
Languages never became the norm in literature – thus
Different from most of Africa and still that way today.

Far more known then (and known more now, even after all this
        time)
Was the armed struggle of Eritrea for independence:
Not that its languages ever strayed from the indigenous.
Nevertheless, Ngũgĩ wrote two decades after his "farewell,"
2006, after reading Eritreans translated:
"Four thousand years…from the ancient stele in Belew Kelew to
20th-century battlefields…into the 21st…"
Poets from there never gave "up writing in their…languages."
Therefore, "their poetry thrives." He knew because he went
        there twice.

Early December in 1998 he visited

For the first time as an introduction yet in connection
With a big conference he agreed to lead, "Against All Odds":
Focused on African languages and literatures, named
With the same phrase often used to brand the Eritrean war
For independence, an all but hopeless, protracted struggle.
Ngũgĩ, of course, was adverse to hype and thought the phrase
     too much
Without the "languages" part. He even said, when I asked him,
"Heinemann's treated me rather well and has served African
Europhone writers well, too. But if the phrase applies to the
Struggle of African language writers it might not be an
Exaggeration." In Eritrea, all the writers used
African languages – "with our fathers, the Italians
As the exception," the joke said. Therefore, Ngũgĩ and "Ertra"
Seemed like a match made in heav…or better, Africa itself.

Zemhret Yohannes, the Eritrean leader in culture
Hosted his travel, and Kassahun Checole, the publisher,
Made the trip happen and flew with Ngũgĩ from America.
On this first visit, again the war between Eritrean
And Ethiopian armies stalked the Horn, but *"Quale guerra"*?
Asked people in Eritrea's biggest city, Asmara.
Nor did the war appear elsewhere as he traveled the country:
Not, at least, this war. The pockmarked walls, abandoned
     armor, and
Regular rubble in piles evoked too many past battles.

All of the wars past and war now might have passed through
     Ngũgĩ's mind
On the Massawa beach where he sat enthralled by the Red Sea.
Other than war what else could have kept him staring out so
     long?
All of the people who knew him in Asmara on the street –
Saying hello as if he was also their greatest writer?

Meeting the president and, perhaps, the inescapably
Flickering visions of Kenya's president in the room, too?
Leaving Asmara, the drive down the escarpment through the
    clouds:
Almost two miles the descent through mountains terraced with
    peace and
Families meeting him there, embracing him as their own and
In their own languages, showing him the schools they have
    rebuilt
And the remains of their ancient farms: the orange trees, coffee,
Black pepper bushes, and even an old pool faintly turquoise?

When he beheld the Red Sea and didn't move for a long time,
Did he imagine, as he would later write, himself a bird
Flying among the divinities all over Africa:
Egypt, Zimbabwe, Meroë, and Aksum, before landing here?
Touching warm waters where Moses, Jesus, and Mohammed
    fled
Their persecution to save their faiths that later changed the
    world?
Nearby Adulis the ancient port of ships to the land of
Punt, camel caravans seeming endless, and monasteries
Where monks of Red Sea gods mastered arts of preserving the
    dead
Thousands of years without rotting? Also, when weren't there
    the wars?
Conquest, repression, and occupation; and the resistance;
Blood feuds among kin and kith? The bird he thought of as
    himself
Flew up a valley so steep and deep the ancient Sahos said
Time had begun there, and just a little further stood a stele –
Lonely, defiant – dark spike of respite in blinding sunlight.
Landing he pecked, that is, read, and locals buzzed in
    amazement,

Seeing the bird make itself at home deciphering the text.
What did it say? – part Sabean letters, older than Ge'ez.
"Wars…the impossible…maybe…struggle…always…odds…
     against…."
Then he flew north to a town called Segeneyti, where he found
Wordmongers gathered beneath the monumental sycamores.

Thirteen months later, to start the new millennium, Ngũgĩ
Came back a second time to Asmara. What would he say to
Hundreds of writers and scholars, students, activists, artists,
Civic groups, NGOs, educators, from throughout the world,
Joining the thousands of Eritrean citizens there, too,
Focused on African language art for seven days and nights?
"Both as an African and a writer, this is certainly
One of the happiest days of my life." Ngũgĩ's opening
Words to the crowd sounded personal, continuing, "Half my
Writing life was taken up by English, even though my books
Were about Kenya and Kenyan people." But the second half,
"From 1977 to the present," Ngũgĩ said,
Changing his tone, "I have written in Gĩkũyũ" – declaring
He was a part of yet totally amazed at how many
Writers in African languages came together before him,
More overwhelmed by their presence and by where they all
     came from
Than by his suddenly seeing his ideas happen right there:
Doing for African languages what all intellectuals
Have done for theirs, which he slowly and forthrightly called
     "The best
[w]ritten and thought in the world." The spearhead of the
     conference
Had to be Ngũgĩ, but it was joining more than leading that,
He said years later, amazed him: "We were…in Eritrea…
Writers…primarily…all there…who wrote in their African

Eritrea, 2002, photo by Lawrence F. Sykes, courtesy of Lawrence F. Sykes.

Languages, and it was beautiful to see. I was writing
Novels and published a journal in the Gĩkũyũ language."

More of this kind of communion happened to him when the
    play,
Translated from the Gĩkũyũ, *Ngaahika Ndeenda*,
By his own hand into English, *I Will Marry When I Want,*
Had its premiere in the Cinema Asmara, translated
Into Tigrinya. Enthralled, he could be seen saying the lines
In their Gĩkũyũ or English matching the new translation.
"Somehow he got it," said Alemseged Tesfai, translator
And Eritrea's most expert, eloquent historian
At the conclusion, the theater's red walls blazing in stage lights,
Actors and audience rushed each other. Kenyan flags, Mau
    Mau
Songs in Tigrinya, and muses painted in the cupola
By a colonial artist who, of course, was Italian,
Freely got lost in each other, and it was total pleasure.
Later the play in Tigrinya toured all over the country.
Seen in the high schools and all the major towns, *I Will Marry
When I Want* has reinforced the drama of Eritrea.
Mes tabarhāni 'emer'o – Ngũgĩ loved the production.

Next day he met with the organizers of the conference,
Planning a statement on what it really meant and the outcome.
Berbere tagliatelle and a little wine sparked discussion.
Ngũgĩ began a preamble, writing on an envelope
He wouldn't show me when I peered over, hoping for a peek.
Later a plenary session gathered all the conferees,
Making suggestions for what we should say. Hundreds of
    people
Spoke from the floor and delivered it in writing one by one
Into the hands of the organizers sitting on the stage.
Three hours later they wearily retreated to compose –

What would become the Asmara Declaration – handwritten
Back in a storage room near the hotel auditorium
And the result of our egolessly following Ngũgĩ
Humbly compressing his twenty years of African language
Ideas and writing to improvise some basic principles
We could agree on – some edits and a few more added, too.
Three hours later we came out with a declaration of
African languages independence. I recall Ngũgĩ
Saying this outcome now settled, once and for all, the language
Question in Africa. Later that night at a huge banquet
Spread in Asmara's art deco city hall, the conferees
Listened to all of the declaration read aloud and cheered.
Asked if they'd ratify what it said, they roared back one big
    "Yes!"
Exhilaration and Eritrean music and dancers
Bursting on stage, the crowd joined them, leaving very little
    room.
Still Ngũgĩ joined, so I joined him, standing by Papa Susso
Playing his kora along with Sbrit, the Eritrean troupe.
Dancing we laughed when an Eritrean businessman, his tie
Flying behind him ran up and pasted one hundred nakfa
On Ngũgĩ's forehead and pasted bills on Papa and me, too.

As for the wordmongers gathered under huge sycamore trees,
I was there also when ancient Eritrean mothers saw
Ngũgĩ and gave him the special bread they baked for his
    coming;
And when they told him to break the loaves so everyone would
    eat.

If a term like "the heroic" still has any use today,
It can describe Eritrea's revolution and struggle
For independence, but seeing Ngũgĩ in Eritrea,
I call it "minor heroic," and write dactylic hexameters,

One of the oldest prosodic rhythms of my language kingdom.

Minor Origins: Adulis

Not DNA or the parents, parents' parents – that kind of
    bloodline.
I mean the mind – hence, the "minor" – I can embrace as my
    own:
Half picking up why an ancient place has been destroyed and
    half
Picking up where shallow canyons gashed by seasonal rivers
Dragged it to sea or then buried what remained, a mile from
    shore,
Where I stand now: half forgetting – or how could life
    continue? –
And half remembering.   If not that at least, what could be
    worse:
Stuck with oblivion covered by geology; at best
Seeing a million-year-old skull but without a history?
Let it be minor, I don't care. I can live in my mind there.

From almost anywhere might describe the people of this place –
Color and shade and belief exchange each other as they like:
Same with their languages; multi-, poly-, with lots of cognates
Tumbling uncertainly in and out of each other's scripts with
No pre- or post- and no centric. Let this place also set free
Time from the one-way unyielding arrow faster and faster.

To the defiance of precedent and to the beautiful....
Fanciful history, half-forgotten and half remembered –
Can it be alien and indigenous at the same time?
All in the mind – minor origins, admittedly, but see

Pieces of it on the surface: alabaster chips pried off
Columns, obsidian tool bits, potsherds littering the sand;
From no one time or place but brought here to stay for as long
     as
More floods and more fire will let them: minor origins also
Dug from the soil of volcanoes and beneath the small, grazed
     hills
Scattered with shrubs and worn paths; a wall, a temple,
     someone's house –
Layers and layers atop each other, as usual, too,
Until they stop. But what happens? What consigns them to
     minor,
If not forever, then at least as long as I'll ever know?
What stops the malachite pigment and the pulverized lapis

Lazuli, laced with pure gold? What stops the greatest poem yet
Finding its home here, with commentary and the images
Of the invisible and divine made visible and flesh?
Who says the bracelet of thorns and bunch of nails for a child
Must not be platinum, only real? Original stone floors
Ripple with answers I rub my hands across and only see
More minor origins waking the imaginary in
Slashes for windows in corrugated walls stuffed with burlap,
Branches, and sticks stuck to cast off lumber and plastic
     tarpaulins.
Off in the distance an archway opens into another –

Archways and archways where someone seeming like an
     immortal

Disappears walking. I see it happen, and similarly
I see an elegant staircase curving into empty air.
At the same moment I find a little grinding stone and trace
Its indentations like definitions of the word "prevail."
It's all around me, too, seeming minor. What else could it be?
Inhuman skyline with no tradition or with every trope
Stripped off your body by strangers or your people all the
     same?
Here they come railing, condemning, burning, violent,
     thronging,
Featureless, equally lost up close or distant in vague light:

Weapon on weapon, the only chance to stand and fight and fall;
Every representation of a blindfolded woman
Weighing the justice of any such scene in her scales pulled
     down –
Broken in pieces: the minor origins will be made real:
Crushed and abased as if sorrow, torture, triumph, and order
Built a vast dam to hold back a constant, much greater power:
Concrete poured deep, holding monumental turbines to set free
Only what's needed: like seeing minor origins to me.
Look at the lilacs to pick behind the house that's abandoned.
Look at that covered up woman spelling K I S S….

Adulis, 2019, photo by Abraham Zerai, courtesy of Abraham Zerai.

Notes

The Woodstock Sandal

Page 1

Woodstock

Outdoor rock and roll music festival of unprecedented proportions and social and personal influence held on a farm in upstate New York, August 15-18, 1969, with an estimated crowd of 400,000 people.

West Orange

Town in northeastern New Jersey and a suburb of Newark.

Newark

City in northeastern New Jersey and the state's largest.

Washington University

Large private research university in St. Louis, Missouri, founded in 1853.

Hemingway, Ernest

(1899-1961). Major American novelist, journalist, short story writer, and Nobel Prize winner in 1954; famous for his concise, incisive style and sharp focus on America, Europe, Africa, war, and adventure.

Fitzgerald, F. Scott

(1896-1940). Major American novelist and short story writer of the "Lost Generation" and famous for his portrayals of high society, lush excess, and self-destruction in American society during the Jazz Age of the 1920s.

The Beatles
(1960-1970). English rock and roll quartet from Liverpool whose music was the most popular, original, and beloved of its time.

Revolver
The Beatles' seventh album released in 1966 and notable for its experimental advances on traditional rock and roll and the Beatles' previous recordings.

Sgt. Pepper's Lonely Hearts Club Band
The Beatles' eighth album released in 1967 and widely acclaimed as the group's greatest collection of songs, fusing lyrical intensity with experimental composition and sound.

Cream
(1966-1970).   English rock and roll trio and seminal supergroup, distinguished by its members' uniquely high-powered musicianship and success in other bands while drawing heavily on traditional rhythm and blues for a new sound termed "psychedelic."

Hendrix, Jimi
(1942-1970). American rock and roll guitarist, singer, and songwriter whose bold and experimental, lyrical intensity resounded with a traditional sense of rhythm and blues that became foundational as psychedelic music.

"The Waste Land"
(1922). Long, erudite, experimental, and highly acclaimed poem by American yet England-based poet, T.S. Eliot (1888-1965), whose work was considered the most influential in 20th-century poetry and literary criticism.

Tweed
> Thick, rough woven fabric in mostly muted colors; used for jackets, suits, dresses, hats, and more, and associated with British Isles.

Paisley
> Decorative and usually colorful pattern of teardrop shapes with curved tails and similar geometric motifs of Middle Eastern origin.

Day-Glo
> Colors so extremely bright that they are fluorescent.

bell bottoms
> Pants worn by men and women that billowed or "belled" from the knee down.

The Who
> (1964-). English rock and roll quartet whose hard-driving, powerful, raw yet refined and original music would reach such a pitch of intensity that the group would destroy its instruments and equipment while performing.

Jefferson Airplane
> (1965-1972). Rock and roll quintet from San Francisco whose distinct sound of female lead vocals, strong harmonies, lyrical musicianship, rhythmic drive, and frequently surreal lyrics made them another major band in psychedelic music.

"Somebody to Love"
> One of Jefferson Airplane's most popular songs, released in 1967 and written by Darby Slick.

Page 2

Union City
> Overlooking the Hudson River and New York City in northeastern New Jersey; an old manufacturing town and a home for many waves of immigrants to the United States.

Fillmore East

(1968-1971). Historic Yiddish theater on New York City's lower East Side that became the most prestigious and famous venue of the greatest rock and roll bands of the era.

East Village

Geographically the East side of lower Manhattan and of Greenwich Village, which together formed a neighborhood and was considered the home of New York City's popular counterculture from the 1950s to recent times.

Blind Faith

(1969). English rock and roll band and supergroup, two of whose members came from Cream, bringing along their high-powered musicianship yet tempering its psychedelia with English soul and folk music.

Clapton, Eric

(1945-). English rock and roll and blues guitarist of towering yet mercurial musicianship with a unique mastery of a variety of genres as well as the founder and leader of many of the most successful bands in his time.

Baker, Ginger

(1939-2019). English drummer and co-founder of Cream and Blind Faith, after which he concentrated more on jazz and African drumming.

Winwood, Stevie

(1948-). English singer / keyboardist and distinctively high tenor in many styles – rhythm and blues, hearty rock and roll, and gentle ballads – and many bands, including Spenser Davis Group (1963-1967), Traffic (1967-1969), and Blind Faith.

Madison Square Garden

Name of a multi-purpose arena built and rebuilt in several Manhattan locations and finally rebuilt and opened in midtown Manhattan in 1968 on the site of the historic Penn Station, which was torn down, although the railroad station remained functioning below.

VW bus
> Volkswagen's longstanding 9-passenger van, bus, or minibus that became iconic in the 1960s and 70s as a "hippie van."

Newport
> Historic city and summer resort on the coast of Rhode Island and identified with wealth, yachting, and mansions and the site of the Newport Jazz Festival, established in 1954.

Atlantic City Pop
> Outdoor contemporary music festival that took place at the Atlantic City Race Course or horse track, August 1-3, 1969, with a roster of musicians comparable to Woodstock's.

John the Baptist
> In the Bible, New Testament prophet and preacher who appeared in 1st-century Judea and who, baptizing masses of people (Mark 1:4-5) is considered Jesus' immediate and prophetic forerunner.

Page 3

Holme
> (1970-). New Jersey rock and roll band distinguished by its mainstream set lists and longstanding popularity particularly as a bar and party band in northern New Jersey and the Jersey shore.

Page 4

"Are You Experienced"
> One of Jimi Hendrix's most popular songs and the title of his first studio album, released in 1967, which became one of the most notable albums in its time.

Page 5

KLH

(1954-). Founded in Cambridge, MA, KLH Research and Development Corporation produces high quality, portable and standing audio equipment, including the popular Model Eleven, first sold in 1962.

Blakey, Art

(1919-1990). Legendary jazz drummer who performed with most of the leading jazz musicians of his time and was founder of the time-honored Jazz Messengers, in the early 1950s, which launched the careers of many more leading jazz musicians.

Davis, Miles

(1926-1991). The greatest American jazz trumpeter, bandleader, and innovator of the 20th century, who cycled through leading and playing with nearly every major jazz musician of his time and whose mercuriality determined the jazz history of his age.

Hancock, Herbie

(1940-). American jazz keyboardist, bandleader, and composer who joined the famous Miles Davis Quintet in 1963 and whose evolution as a musician represented, encompassed, and largely determined the history of jazz as well as jazz fusion.

Evans, Bill

(1929-1980). American jazz pianist, composer, and progenitor of jazz trios and whose distinctively intense lyrical impressionism and mutability could be traditional and romantic, passionate and intellectual, innovative and classic.

Page 6

Blood, Sweat, and Tears

(1967-1981). Canadian-American group who blended rock and roll, blues, and jazz with a heavy mixture of brass and complex arrangements and instrumentation.

Ten Years After

(1966-1970). English band devoted to playing blues with the intensity of high powered rock and roll and the transfixing lead guitar and vocals of Alvin Lee.

Beck, Jeff

(1944-). English rock and roll lead guitarist who combined maximum musicianship with fretboard pyrotechnics comparable to and often playing in bands that prior to his joining had featured other guitar greats, Eric Clapton and Jimmy Page.

Led Zeppelin

(1968-1980). English rock band of such extraordinary power and intensity – instrumentally and vocally – combined with intoxicating and erotic lyricism that it originated and propagated its own massive sound that became known as "heavy metal."

Sly and the Family Stone

(1966-1983). San Francisco-based American band, male and female, black and white, led by Sly Stone, who wrote, performed, and produced a uniquely musical and potent blend of rock and funk, soul and psychedelia, and rhythm and blues.

Coltrane, John

(1926-1967). Supreme and innovative American jazz player of saxophone whose compositions, improvisations, originality, and development from traditional sideman to founder of the John Coltrane Quartet spawned free jazz and a legacy of unparalleled and unequaled brilliance and creativity.

Tyner, McCoy
(1938-2020). American jazz pianist, composer, and band leader whose driving yet shimmering musicality illuminated the John Coltrane Quartet and half a century more of acoustic and richly transcendent piano performance.

Sanders, Pharoah
(1940-). American jazz saxophone player who emerged from performing with John Coltrane to become an innovative often spell-binding soloist in his own bands, featuring quasi-spiritual melodies, powerful "sheets of sound", and African rhythms and instruments.

...alles Fleish, es ist wie Gras
German, "all flesh is grass," Isaiah 40:6.

Brahms, Johannes
(1833-1897). German composer, pianist, and conductor whose symphonies, chamber music, and more exhibited and matched the greatness of his two greatest predecessors, Johann Sebastian Bach and Ludwig van Beethoven, along with unprecedented innovation.

Ein Deutsches Requiem (A German Requiem)
A traditional work of music to commemorate the dead, composed by Johannes Brahms over the years 1865-1868 in seven movements and among the gravest, most monumental, and redemptive musical statements ever made on human mortality.

Dionysius
Ancient Greek god, named Bacchus by the Romans, associated with wine, fertility, religious ecstasy and madness, feasting, frenzy, and extreme pleasure bordering on chaos.

The Rolling Stones
(1962-). Longstanding if not immortal bearers of the claim, "the world's greatest rock and roll band," consisting of five Englishmen whose original compositions, renditions of traditional blues, performances, recordings, and critical recognition are unsurpassed.

Pärt, Arvo
(1935-). Original, prolific, Estonian composer of classical music in many genres that are infused with spirituality and redolent with medieval Catholic as well as Orthodox religiosity and musical forms transformed into 20th-century Minimalism.

Reich, Steve
(1936-). Major American composer whose percussive, harmonic, pulsing, and distinctively recurring musical patterns in a variety of musical genres extend to include a wide range of cultural resources from the Old Testament to modern American poetry.

Tavener, John
(1944-2013). English composer whose lyrical, spiritual, intense, and often Minimalist works derive heavily from medieval and Renaissance European sacred music while embodying classical music that thrives in contemporary, secular contexts.

Adams, John Luther
(1953-). American composer critically and widely recognized for his music's expression, identification, and seemingly bonding with the dramatic and monumental power of nature autonomous of human nature in the American West from Alaska to Mexico.

Adams, John
(1947-). Major and prolific American composer of symphonies, opera, chamber music, and more that range

from and synthesize Mahler-like to Minimalist musical tropes and orchestration often relating to modern and post-modern historical events.

Lang, David

(1957-).   American composer and second-generation Minimalist based in New York City and whose ensembles and collaborations exemplify an original, classical, melodic, harmonic, and influential synthesis of contemporary culture and lyrical gravitas.

Page 7

Yin Yang

Ancient Chinese philosophical symbol of a circle with two contiguous and dovetailed droplets, light and dark, that represent cosmological dualism, dynamism, and complementarity.

The Fugs

American rock and roll band from New York City with a rough and ready, uniquely counter-cultural brand of obscenity, comedy, and anti-Vietnam war sentiment.

Gallo

E & J Gallo Winery, founded in California in 1933 and major exporter of California wines, most of which are low priced and basic in taste.

Mulligan, Gerry

(1927-1996).   Renowned American saxophone player, composer, band leader, and arranger especially admired for his jazz artistry on the baritone saxophone that epitomized a blithe and unbothered style known as "cool jazz."

Brubeck, Dave

(1920-2012). Popular and influential jazz pianist, composer, and group leader whose compositions propelled "cool jazz" and American jazz itself further into the mainstream of American music than ever before.

Burton, Gary

(1943-). American jazz vibraphone player, composer, group leader, and educator whose innovative technique and distinctively singular yet reverberating tones became the standard for vibraphone in jazz as well as in jazz fusion.

Page 8

Dubois, W. B. E.

(1868-1963). American writer, scholar, critic, editor, cultural activist, and Pan-Africanist; co-founder of the National Association for the Advancement of Colored People (NAACP) and the Pan-African Congress; the leading intellectual and most influential African American of his time.

Vietnam War

Armed conflict between North and South Vietnam in which, from the early 1960s, the United States became heavily involved in combat until massive American fatalities eventually over 55,000 provoked widescale protest: enough to force a major American military withdrawal by 1972 and total communist North Vietnam victory in 1975.

Newark riots

Riots to the point of a full-scale rebellion that took place in downtown Newark NJ, July 12-17, 1967, pitting inner-city African Americans against a largely white police force and national guard, resulting in extensive looting, property destruction, hundreds of people injured, and twenty-six fatalities.

Page 10

Galaxy

Large, well-equipped, high-end car built by the Ford Motor Company from 1959 to 1974.

Jones, Leroi, aka Baraka, Amiri
> (1934-2014). Poet, essayist, dramatist, novelist, and cultural activist based in Newark NJ, whose Black Nationalism in the 1960s and 70s and constant literary output analyzing and attacking racism made him one of the most important American writers of his time.

ROTC
> The Reserve Officer Training Corps, a program at many American colleges and universities, providing students with training so that upon graduation they could become commissioned officers in the US armed forces.

Page 11

Joplin, Janis
> (1943-1970). Singer and songwriter born in Texas whose passionate and uniquely powerful blend of rock and roll, blues, and soul both on recordings and, even more, on stage made her an inimitable, iconic performer of the era.

Big Brother and the Holding Company
> (1965-1972). American band that hailed from and typified San Francisco rock and roll music culture of the time, with Janis Joplin as lead singer.

"Try (Just a Little Bit Harder)"
> Rousing yet funky first song on the album, *I Got Dem Ol' Kozmic Blues Again Mama*, released in 1969 and featuring Janis Joplin as lead singer of a blues and soul-based band, including horns.

Stone, Sly
> (1943-). American singer, songwriter, instrumentalist, and co-founder, with Cynthia Robinson, of Sly and the Family Stone, a large group with a powerful mix of rock, soul, and gospel that was new and influential in the development of psychedelic music.

Page 12

YouTube

Online and seemingly limitless video collection and sharing platform founded in California in 2005.

Spotify

Online music streaming service founded in Sweden in 2006 with a vast catalogue of selections from all genres.

R & B

Meaning "rhythm and blues," a genre of African American music going back to the 1940s, at least, in which traditional blues expands to include increased dynamic and varied rhythm and instrumentation, more often than not electrified.

Page 13

Little Richard

(1932-2020). American soul singer, songwriter, and pianist from Georgia whose compositions in the 1950s became bedrock rock and roll and whose performance style embodied extravagance and color utterly unique, uninhibited, inimitable, and always musical.

Mitchell, Joni

(1943-). Proto singer-songwriter from Canada whose guitar compositions and poetic lyrics expressed musical origins in folk, pop, and jazz through a mezzo soprano, vibrato-tinged voice that grappled with youthful and existential love and disillusionment.

"Woodstock"

Popular song by Joni Mitchell about the music festival and released in 1970, the most famous recording of which was by Crosby, Stills, Nash & Young in the same year.

Daltrey, Roger
>(1944-). Lead singer and co-founder of the Who, whose strong and wide-ranging voice and dynamic body movement in performance embodied a kind of unassailable power.

Townsend, Pete
>(1945-). The Who's co-founder, leader, songwriter, vocalist, and guitarist whose compositions, musicality, and originality blended primitive power and distinctive sophistication to create a high quality and commercial appeal triumphant in his arm-wheeling power chords.

Havens, Richie
>(1941-2013). American singer-songwriter and guitarist whose strong strumming and raspy voice made his blend of folk music and soul achieve mantra-like proportions.

Cocker, Joe
>(1944-2014). English singer whose covers of his era's hit songs were unique for his gravelly yet often tender vocal inflections combined in performance with his spasmodic body movements.

Page 14

"The Star-Spangled Banner"
>The national anthem of the United States, lyrics by Francis Scott Key (1779-1843), music by John Stafford Smith (1759-1836), played by Jimi Hendrix on solo electric guitar, 8/19/69, to conclude the Woodstock festival.

LGBT
>Popular acronym – standing for Lesbian, Gay, Bisexual, Transgender – coined in the wake of contemporary social and political progress in recognition and respect for sexual self-identification.

Page 15

Susser, Ernie

> Music store owner and record producer in Newark NJ, from
> ca. 1950s to 1980s.

Weequahaic

> Neighborhood in Newark NJ's south ward, which was
> mostly middle-class Jewish from World War II to the 1960s.

Roth, Philip

> (1933-2018). Major novelist and short story writer whose
> fiction often focuses on his birthplace, Newark NJ, veiled
> autobiography, sexuality, and Jewish American life.

Page 16

Volunteers

> Album and eponymous song released by the Jefferson
> Airplane in 1969.

Kent State

> Large public university founded in 1910 in Kent OH, where
> on May 4, 1970 the Ohio National Guard killed four and
> wounded nine students by firing into an unarmed crowd
> protesting the Vietnam war.

Crosby, Stills, Nash & Young

> (1968-1971). David Crosby, Stephen Stills, Graham Nash,
> and Neil Young supergroup derived from each member's
> prowess and high powered musicality in previous bands,
> resulting in an electrified, shimmering rock sound laced with
> folk strains, which gained enormous, lasting popularity.

"Ohio"

> Hit song released by Crosby, Stills, Nash & Young in 1971
> that protested and commemorated the killings at Kent State
> University in 1970.

Jackson State

Historically black, public university founded as Natchez Seminary in 1877 in Mississippi, where city and state police on May 14, 1970, opened fire, killing two and injuring four in a crowd of students protesting the Vietnam war.

Alighieri, Dante

(1265-1321). Italian poet, literary and philosophical writer whose choice to write his greatest work, the epic poem, *Commedia* – popularly known as *Divina Commedia* and *The Divine Comedy* – in his vernacular language instead of classical Latin and in the poetic form of *terza rima* radically changed the course of European literary history.

Ciardi, John

(1916-1986). Popular and highly skilled American poet and translator whose translation of Dante's *Divine Comedy*, in a modified *terza rima*, was one of the most widely read and assigned translations in English.

terza rima

Poetic form of three-line stanzas or triplets that rhyme aba bcb cdc ded efe...etc.

Page 18

"Pleasant Valley Sunday"

Popular song by Carole King and Gerry Goffin, recorded by the Monkees in 1967 and evoking suburban life on and around Pleasant Valley Way, a major road in West Orange NJ.

King, Carole

(1942-). Popular song writer and singer of many hits and albums whose accomplished, lyrical, polished, and immediately accessible and identifiable style made her one of the most successful musical artists of her time.

The Beats

A group of post-World War II writers also known as the Beat Generation whose alienation from mainstream conservative American culture celebrated protest, anti-materialism, nonconformity, alternative spirituality, sexual freedom, hedonism, and alleged deviance.

radical leftism

A political orientation highly critical of mainstream conservative American policies and governance yet similarly disparaging of its liberal counterparts for their tolerance of capitalism and moderation in confronting problems of race, class, and gender.

Black Nationalism

Political, social, and racial orientation stemming from early 20th-century America and powerfully revived in the 1960s by the Black Power, Black Panther, and Nation of Islam movements as well as by black writers, artists, musicians, and cultural activists.

Canterbury

Small city in the county of Kent in southeastern England, famous as a medieval pilgrimage and cathedral site while also being the headquarters of the Anglican Church.

Shakespeare

(1564-1616). Poet and dramatist, England's and the English language's greatest writer, and the author of thirty-nine plays and many more poems of untold influence and popularity while he also became a leading literary entrepreneur in his time.

"Sympathy for the Devil"

Hit song composed by Mick Jagger and Keith Richard of the Rolling Stones and released by the group in 1968.

Dover

Port town in England's southeastern county of Kent and famous for its white cliffs abutting the English Channel.

King Lear

Tragic drama by William Shakespeare, written in 1605 or 1606, and charting the decline and destruction of a king who retires from his throne and divides his kingdom among his three daughters with the direst consequences, including all of their deaths.

Edgar

In Shakespeare's *King Lear*, the honest and long-suffering, legitimate son of the king's aged, principal advisor, the Earl of Gloucester.

Keswick

Major town in northwest England's "Lake District," well-known for its natural beauty, and where Romantic 19th-century poets William Wordsworth (1770-1850) and Samuel Taylor Coleridge (1772-1834) lived and wrote.

Page 19

Keats, John

(1795-1821). Major English Romantic poet whose odes, lyric, and narrative poems are uniquely commanding and inspiring for their imagery, rhythmic and emotional intensity, and exactitude.

Spenser, Edmund

(1552-1599). Major Elizabethan lyric and narrative poet unprecedented and unequaled in English literary history for his extensive, bordering on extravagant employment of meter, rhyme, and poetic form.

The Faerie Queene

Epic poem by Edmund Spenser first published in 1590 and distinguished for its stanzaic form, allegory, musicality, stylized language, and episodic portrayal of various knights in the service of traditional Christian virtues.

Machault, Guillaume de
(1300-1377). French poet and composer foremost in his time as an exemplar of the *Ars Nova* movement, which developed polyphonic music to an extraordinary capacity.

Firenze
Known as Florence in English, located in the province of Tuscany in north central Italy and one of its most important cities for art, letters, and commerce in the late Middle Ages and the Renaissance.

The Prelude
Epic autobiographical poem (1805, 1850) by William Wordsworth and subtitled, "Growth of a Poet's Mind."

Chartres
One of France's greatest cathedrals, located ca. 50 miles southwest of Paris, substantially constructed in the late 12th and early 13th centuries.

Siena
City in the Italian province of Tuscany that was politically powerful and a center of the arts in medieval and Renaissance Italy, when it also rivaled Florence.

Di Buoninsegna, Duccio
(ca. 1255 to ca. 1318). Major Italian painter based in Siena and whose monumental achievements fostered a style that expanded Byzantine and medieval art and iconography to develop a groundwork for unparalleled Renaissance innovation.

Louvre
A vast and historic art museum in Paris, located in the Louvre Palace on the banks of the Seine.

Monteverdi, Claudio
    (1567-1643). Major Italian composer and musician whose
    innovative and large scale sacred and secular works,
    including operas, musically mirrored each other and
    distinctively defined their era and locale, especially Venice.

Nietzsche, Friedrich
    (1844-1900). German philosopher whose work with its
    strong and seductive, if sometimes nihilistic style and content
    emphasized the power of dramatic, dynamic, and often
    outrageous statement more than philosophical systems.

Casaubon, Edward
    Character in *Middlemarch* who aspires to an all-encompassing
    and universal acquisition and understanding of knowledge
    and fails.

Middlemarch
    Major English novel published in 1871 by George Eliot
    (aka Mary Ann Evans, 1819-1880) and distinguished for its
    incisive and profound philosophical, social, political, and
    personal analysis as well as its literary realism.

Kerry
    County in southeastern Ireland renowned for its rugged,
    spectacular yet enchanting sea- and landscape.

Athos
    Mountain-peninsula with many ancient monasteries in
    northeastern Greece and the center of Greek Orthodox
    Christianity for thousands of years.

Page 20

Trecento
    Italian word for the fourteenth century and applied to the art
    and culture of the time.

Maestá
> Sequence of forty-three paintings of tempera and gold that form a wooden altarpiece created by Duccio de Buoninsegna in early *trecento* Siena, and his most largescale work.

Derrida, Jacques
> (1930-2004). French philosopher and literary scholar whose general if difficult theory of "deconstruction," detaching and reconnecting texts and their meaning, dominated post-structural and postmodern thinking.

Foucault, Michel
> (1926-1984). French philosopher and social historian whose writings on the connection of power and knowledge dramatically and disturbingly highlighted the use and misuse of the latter to obtain and enforce, often violently, the former.

de Chardin, Teilhard
> (1881-1955). French theologian, paleontologist, and Jesuit priest whose provocative, inspiring, and extensive writings speculated profoundly on the development and evolution of the human mind and spirit in a distinctively Roman Catholic context.

Augustine
> (354 -430). Roman and African doctor, bishop, and father of the Church, author of the revolutionary-for-its-time, autobiographical *Confessions* (ca. 398) and later of the voluminous *City of God* (*De Civitate Dei*), two milestones in Western consciousness.

Benedict
> (ca. 480-547). Father of monasticism in Western and Eastern Christianity and of the Benedictine order and whose brief book or "Rule" outlines proper monastic life.

Bernard of Clairvaux
> (1090-1153).   French monk and abbot who revived the Benedictine order, founded the Cistercians, and wrote many sermons and commentaries, including on the *Song of Songs*.

Mass
> The Catholic and some Protestant and Orthodox churches' most fundamental and frequent form to celebrate their liturgy and the ritual of the Eucharist.

Page 21

St. Catherine's Monastery
> One of the world's most ancient and continuing monasteries, built in the 6th century near Mount Sinai and containing equally ancient artifacts and books.

Bar Mitzvah
> Jewish ritual for boys to mark and celebrate their entering manhood.

West Bank
> Historic, biblical land that is west of the Jordan River and, although claimed by Israel and Palestine, considered home by both, ruled mostly by Israel.

Bethlehem
> Historic birthplace of Jesus Christ and even more ancient yet continuing city located in the West Bank.

Nablus
> Ancient and continuing city in the West Bank and frequent flashpoint of Palestinian / Israeli conflict.

Joseph
> Favorite, youngest, and eleventh son of biblical patriarch, Jacob, and who, sold into slavery by his envious brothers, rose to be the second most powerful man in Pharaonic Egypt, at which time he emotionally reconciled with his family.

Hebron

Ancient, largest and continuing city in the West Bank, business center and renowned burial place of Abraham, Isaac, Jacob, and their wives – Sara, Rebecca, and Rachel – in the Cave of the Patriarchs, situated in the mosque / synagogue at the center of the city.

Page 22

Dead Sea

Bordering Israel and Jordan, large lake south of Jerusalem and with a high level of salt that dictates a harsh environment while providing uniquely enjoyable aquatic activity.

Jericho

Most ancient and continuing West Bank city, close to Jordan, and dating back to the ninth century BCE.

Qumran

Arid, harsh, marl (sedimentary clay and lime) plateau and cliffs in the West Bank and near the northwestern shore of the Dead Sea.

Suez Canal

Opened in 1869, a man-made waterway that connects the Mediterranean and the Red Sea.

National Museum

The Museum of Egyptian Antiquities in downtown Cairo near Tahrir Square.

Page 23

Horus

Ancient Egyptian god of the sky and signified with a falcon.

Anubis

Ancient Egyptian god of the dead and signified with a jackal.

Ptah

Ancient Egyptian god who is a creator, maker, and artist.

Thoth
> Ancient Egyptian god associated with writing and signified with the head of an ibis or a baboon.

Seshat
> Ancient Egyptian female god of the word, measure, and books.

Osiris
> Ancient Egyptian god and ruler of the dead, life, and the afterlife.

Orpheus
> Ancient Greek mythological musician and poet whose art in the natural world had mysterious, supernatural powers.

Eurydice
> Beautiful woman whose life her husband, Orpheus, tried to saved but failed by descending to hell to find her and bring her back to life on earth.

Between Shores

Page 25

"Build Me Up Buttercup"
> Popular song released by the Foundations in 1968.

"My Back Pages"
> Song written by Bob Dylan (1941-) and a hit in 1967 by the Byrds (1964-1973), an American rock and roll band distinctive for its leader, Roger McGuinn, playing electric 12-string guitar.

"Walk Away Renee"
> Hit song in 1966 with refined vocals and orchestration by the Left Banke.

"Gloria"
> Hit song written by Van Morrison that, when it was released by Them in 1965, became wildly popular and recorded and released by many subsequent rock and roll artists.

"Honky Tonk Woman"
> Rolling Stones hit song in 1969 and written by Mick Jagger and Keith Richards.

"Mustang Sally"
> Rhythm and blues hit song recorded and released by major soul singer, Wilson Pickett, in 1966.

"Happy Together"
> Popular song released in 1967 by the American rock group, The Turtles, and their only hit.

Motown
> Motown Records, a recording company that, originating in Detroit – Mo(tor) Town – became the greatest, most innovative and successful producer of soul music through assembling a perennial roster of artists who individually and together established the elemental yet mainstream American Motown Sound.

"Mony, Mony"
> Released in 1968, Tommy James and the Shondells' popular but sole hit song.

Return to Paris

Page 29

Rue de Nesle
> Small street in Paris' sixth arrondissement on the Left Bank and just south of the Pont Neuf.

Starbucks

A coffee company and international coffeehouse chain, founded in Seattle, Washington in 1971.

Page 30

trivium

Latin term of late, classical Roman culture to designate three of the liberal arts, including grammar, logic, and rhetoric.

quadrivium

Latin term of late, classical Roman culture to designate four of the liberal arts, including arithmetic, geometry, music, and astronomy.

Page 31

Notre Dame

Famous and historic medieval cathedral in the center of Paris and the embodiment of French Gothic architecture *par excellence.*

Holy Communion

Also called the Eucharist, the Christian ritual of eating bread and wine in remembrance of the body and blood of Jesus Christ when he was crucified.

Agnus Dei

Latin, "Lamb of God," prayer spoken when the bread of the Eucharist is broken and beheld in Christian liturgy.

Peccata mundi

Latin, "sins of the world," phrase from the *Agnus Dei* prayer.

vicit...sequamur

Latin, "conquer...follow," excerpted from the inscription on the emblem of the Moravian Church: "*Vicit agnus noster, eum sequamur,*" "Our lamb has conquered, let us follow Him."

Un étranger

French, "a stranger."

La mort. C'est moi.

French, "Death. It's me."

Page 32

Seine

River that flows west to east through the middle of Paris.

La Samaritaine

Architecturally iconic and historic, large department store on the Seine and near the Pont Neuf in Paris.

Ars Nova

14th-century French and Italian music considered new for its rhythmic and melodic departures from *Ars Antiqua* or ancient music of the 13th century and before.

Page 33

Demeter

Greek god of agriculture, whose Roman name is Ceres, and mother of Persephone or Proserpina.

Athena

Greek god of wisdom and war, whose Roman name is Minerva, and daughter of no mother but sprung from the head of Zeus.

Gauls

People from Gaul, *Gallia* in Latin, a Roman term to refer to the area of west central Europe.

Gare du Nord

French, Paris North, one of the six biggest train stations in Paris.

Gbago, Laurent

(1945-). President of Côte d'Ivoire from 2000-2011, when he was arrested and removed from office, yet he spent most of the 1980s in exile in Paris.

Edgar Allan Poe in Richmond

Page 35

Edgar Allan Poe

(1809-1849).   One of America's all-time greatest authors: writer of poetry, short stories, a novel, literary criticism, natural science, and extensive correspondence, who was raised in Richmond, Virginia, and whose literary career and unique achievement were largely determined by his life in the American south.

Richmond

Capital of Virginia, capital of the Confederacy during the American civil war and a thriving, contemporary American midsize city.

Cary Street

Central thoroughfare in Richmond's historic district.

4/4

In music, a time signature in which each measure has four quarter notes; most often used in popular music, e.g., rock, blues, country, and funk.

blues

Historic form or genre in American popular music that derives from African American and southern culture while modified in various other regions in the United States, although nearly always, in groups or solo, adhering to the basic blues chord pattern of the first, fourth, and fifth notes in a major scale.

guiro

A musical instrument, usually made of a large gourd, with a serrated surface over which the player runs a stick, called a *pua,* to make a grating noise in various rhythms and patterns.

rapido

Spanish, rapid or fast.

Powhatan

(ca. 1540-1618). Leader or chief of the Powhatan native American tribes, also known as Wahunsenacawh, when English colonists formed and established the Jamestown, Virginia settlement.

Pocahontas

(1596-1617). Wahunsenacawh's storied daughter whom John Smith (1580-1630), Jamestown settler, claimed as his benefactor, and who was captured by English colonists and married to tobacco planter, John Rolfe, with whom she traveled to England.

James River

Virginia's largest river, beginning in the Appalachian Mountains, flowing through Richmond and into Chesapeake Bay.

Page 36

Mordecai, Samuel

(1786-1865). Successful merchant in Richmond VA and a contemporary of Poe.

VA DMV

Virginia Department of Motor Vehicles

Shockoe Bottom

Historic area and one of the oldest neighborhoods in downtown Richmond along the James River.

Page 37

Pantheon

Former Roman temple become a Catholic Church in Rome and distinguished by its massive Corinthian columns, pediment, oculus, and cylindrical shape.

Clemm, Virginia

(1822-1847). Wife of Edgar Allan Poe and related to him on his mother's side.

Page 38

Monumental Church

> Historic, neoclassical, Greek Revival church in Richmond VA, built in 1812 on the site of the Richmond Theatre, which burned on December 26, 1811, killing 72 people.

dactyl

> A three-syllable metrical unit or foot with the first syllable accented or stressed and the second and third syllables unstressed.

trochee

> A two-syllable metrical unit or foot with the first syllable accented or stressed and the second syllable unstressed.

Page 39

Canova

> Antonia Canova (1757-1822), Italian sculptor whose fine, white marble figures aspired to neoclassical perfection.

The Capitol

> Building in Richmond that was originally designed by Thomas Jefferson (1743-1826) to resemble a Roman temple and to serve as Virginia's statehouse, which it still does, while being the first neoclassical building in the New World.

Southern Literary Messenger (SLM)

> The American south's premier literary journal begun in 1834, which Poe edited from December 1835 to January 1837.

Page 40

Milton, John

> (1608-1674). Major English poet and essayist unequalled in his poetry of many genres – including the epic, *Paradise Lost*, and lyric and dramatic – and timely yet timeless political and religious essays.

Christian Sentinel

> Newspaper published in Richmond VA from 1832-1836.

Page 41

Mabbott, Thomas Ollive

>   (1898-1968).   Legendary American scholar and professor who edited the definitive, annotated scholarly edition of Poe's poetry, tales, and sketches.

Eureka

>   Full title, *Eureka: A Prose Poem*, a book length cosmological study published by Poe in 1848.

"He could sing, can 'It...be' me...."

>   "The Flower" (1633) by George Herbert.

>   And now in age I bud again,
>   After so many deaths I live and write;
>   I once more smell the dew and rain,
>   And relish versing: O my only light,
>   It cannot be
>   That I am he
>   On whom thy tempests fell all night.

Whig

>   Variously titled newspaper published in Richmond VA from 1833-1888.

Baltimore

>   Major, historic American port city in Maryland and one of the American cities that Poe lived in.

Page 42

Baudelaire, Charles

>   (1821-1867).   Major and revolutionary French lyric poet, essayist, and translator.

Monte altissimo

>   Latin, high mountain.

Horace
(65-8 BCE). Leading Roman poet whose lyrics exemplified philosophical yet practical understanding, measure, richness, directness, and elegance in expression.

Odes
Quintessential collection of four books of poems by Horace, in Latin titled *Carmina.*

Orris
Iris flower root also used for medicinal uses.

"The Poetic Principle"
1848-1849 essay by Poe, published posthumously in 1850, that became one his most popular lectures, theorizing about length and didacticism in poetry.

"The Raven"
Published in 1845, a highly stylized and rhythmic narrative poem and Poe's most famous in his lifetime and now, with an unforgettable, one-word refrain, "Nevermore," imagined as the utterance of a raven at the poet's door.

Royster, Sarah Elmira
(1810-1888). Romantic interest of Poe as a very young man yet also in the months before he died, when they were engaged.

Exchange Hotel
New and popular hotel in Richmond VA where Poe lectured when he returned to the city, which was his hometown, in 1849.

Talavera's farm
House and property northwest of downtown Richmond where Poe might have given a poetry reading in the summer of 1849.

Norfolk

City ca. 100 miles east of Richmond near the Virginia coast.

"Annabel Lee"

Published in 1849, one of Poe's last poems with "beautiful Annabel Lee," a woman whose death the poet mourns, as a refrain. As Poe also wrote in "The Philosophy of Composition" (1850), "the death...of a beautiful woman is, unquestionably, the most poetical topic in the world."

"Ulalume"

Published in 1847, a ballad by Poe that is distinctive for its diction, rhythm, and allusions in lamenting the death of the poet's beloved.

Page 43

Hollywood Cemetery

Historic and expansive cemetery in Richmond VA, bordered to the south by the James River and containing many Confederate monuments and graves.

Harvey's Woods

Wooded area in 19th-century Richmond VA where Poe played as a child.

Davis, Jefferson

(1808-1869). United States senator from Virginia and president of the Confederate States from (1861-1865) until the end of the Civil War, when the South was defeated.

Crashaw, Richard

(1613-1649). English poet and cleric known for his extravagant religious poetry and who, when he converted to Roman Catholicism, had to flee England and live in Italy, where he briefly ministered at the Shrine of the Holy House in Loreto.

Greenwich Village
> Area in New York City's lower Manhattan that stretches between the Hudson and East rivers, which has been traditionally associated with art and popular culture.

Quinn, Edmond
> (1868-1929). Sculptor famous for his 1908 bust of Poe, a copy of which is on display in the garden shrine of Richmond's Edgar Allan Poe Museum.

Semtner, Chris
> (1975-). Curator, Edgar Allan Poem Museum, scholar and writer on Poe.

At the Grave of Hilda Doolittle (H.D.)

Page 45

Hilda Doolittle (H.D.)
> (1886-1961). Poet, essayist, and novelist, born and buried in Bethlehem PA; among greatest Modernist authors in English and trailblazing women writers of American letters, whose finely wrought work espoused values of Greek classicism, contemporary psychology, sexual freedom, and more.

Page 46

Lehigh River
> Eastern Pennsylvania river that flows from the Appalachian mountains, through Allentown and Bethlehem, and ends in the Delaware River in Easton.

"Lamb who has conquered...etc."
> See "*vicit...sequamur*," 112 (above).

"mute" and "inglorious"
> Excerpted words from Thomas Gray's "Elegy Written in a Country Churchyard" (1751), invoking John Milton and Oliver Cromwell (1599-1658), the poet and the statesman,

respectively, whose poetic prowess and political acumen might have been embodied in a common villager were he in the mainstream and not on the margins of society.

Page 48
Bethlehem
> Small city founded by German Moravians in the mid-18th century in Eastern Pennsylvania and now a thriving part of the state's third most populous region, the Lehigh Valley.

Brutalist
> Style in 20th-century architecture emphasizing mass and geometric shape, including blocks and angles in poured concrete.

Victorian
> Historical era that coincided with the reign of England's Queen Victoria: 1837-1901.

"Sea Rose"
> Short, incisive, imagistic poem by H.D. published in 1916.

Page 49
"Helen"
> Published in 1924, three-stanza, 18-line poem by H.D. about Helen of Troy from the point of view of "Greece," which is personal, classical, imagistic, and nihilistic.

Iliad
> Epic Greek poem in dactylic hexameter by Homer, who may only be legendary, that narrates events that led to the end of the ten-year Trojan War and the Greeks' defeat of Troy, with the poem becoming a model for all subsequent Western epic poems.

"Lovefeast"
> Moravian liturgical service for congregants that includes prayer, hymns, and a communal snack of something made with flour and / or sweet and a nonalcoholic drink.

Moravians

Historic Protestant German and Czech religious deno-
mination begun in the 15th century and active ever since
while extending worldwide.

feminist

Advocate of equal rights and opportunities for women in
all things economic, political, sexual, social, theological, and
anything else.

Freudian

Adherent or relating to the work of Sigmund Freud (1856-
1939), medical doctor and neurologist who founded
psychoanalysis and revolutionized psychology.

Imagiste

Any American or British poet who exemplified the dictum
of Ezra Pound (1885-1972) that a poetic image should be
concise, specific, musical, and stand-alone.

Domicile

Page 55

"The Domain of Arnheim"

Short story published in 1846 by Edgar Allan Poe in which
the main focus is on a garden and landscape that reveal a
balance of art and nature.

Page 56

Proserpina

Latin name for the god of Spring, in Greek, Persephone,
forcibly abducted and taken to the underworld by Pluto
(Hades in Latin), its king.

OCD

Obsessive Compulsive Disorder, a psychological condition of extreme over-concern with the arrangement or order of things.

Nashe, Thomas

(1567-1601). English poet, dramatist, and satirist during the reign of Queen Elizabeth (1533-1603) and buoyant, wily fellow artist of William Shakespeare; author of *Summer's Last Will and Testament* (1592).

"Borne on the bier with"

William Shakespeare, Sonnet 12, 7-8: "And summer's green all girded up in sheaves / Borne on the bier with white and bristly beard."

Page 58

jardin Africain

French, African garden

"Sands"

Casino in Bethlehem PA, 2009-2019, constructed within repurposed buildings once owned by Bethlehem Steel Corporation, founded in Bethlehem in 1904 and declared bankrupt in 2001.

Casamance

Area in southern Senegal separated from the north by the country of Gambia.

Page 59

Maasai

Mostly rural ethnic group and longtime residents in Kenya and northern Tanzania.

Yucatán

Eastern peninsula of Mexico and a state that juts into the Gulf of Mexico.

shida
> Arabic for sandal and storied plastic shoe worn by Eritrean freedom fighters in their war for independence from Ethiopia.

St. Fiacre
> Early medieval Irish saint of varying identities associated with piety, gardens, and misogyny.

Page 61
Hardy, Thomas
> (1840-1928). Major and prolific British author of prose fiction and poems who established himself through the former but throughout his life wrote the latter, often with little stylistic difference over time, yet always with a unique attention to poetic form and rhythm, focusing on a wide range of human character and natural phenomena.

Scholl, Ben
> (1979-). Proprietor of family-owned and operated farming business based in Bethlehem PA.

On a Tree

Page 63
Spenser, Edmund
> See 104 (above).

Page 64
Google Earth
> A computer program with 3D maps and representations of Earth based on satellite images and aerial photography: https://www.google.com/earth/.

von Zinzendorf, Nikolaus Ludwig
> (1700-1760). German Bishop, religious leader, and reformer of the Moravian Church who played an important role in establishing its presence in Bethlehem PA.

Grunewald, Gustav
> (1805-1878). Landscape and portrait painter and teacher from Germany who settled in Bethlehem PA, where he taught and painted.

Page 65

Salix babylonica
> Tree that is popularly known as weeping willow.

Jesse trees
> The tree of Jesse illustration, often found in manuscripts and stained glass windows, featuring the Messiah, Jesus Christ, at the top of a tree, with his ancestors below him and growing out of the loins of Jesse of Bethlehem, the father of David, from whom Jesus is descended, also being born in Bethlehem.

David
> The renowned, ancient king of Israel and the subject of seemingly countless artistic representations.

Page 66

Sycorax
> A powerful witch alluded to as the mother of Caliban and, though neither seen nor heard, imprisoned in a tree by Prospero in Shakespeare's play, *The Tempest* (1610).

Africa Antetranslation

Page 69

Conrad, Joseph

> (1857-1924). Major British novelist born in Poland and a speaker of Polish who learned English, mastered the art of English prose like few others, and wrote a number of novels that often focused on life at sea, travel, and adventure while cultivating a sensibility coterminous with early 20th century-Modernism's political and social disillusion.

Heart of Darkness

> Published in 1899, a novella by Joseph Conrad in which the main character and narrator, Charles Marlowe, embarks on a voyage up the Congo River to find the profoundly compelling and enigmatic Joseph Kurtz, a reputed genius and ivory trader gone rogue.

Page 72

Achebe, Chinua

> (1930-2013). Nigerian novelist, essayist, and poet whose critical stature and role in modern African literature is among the greatest of all African authors, including his first novel, *Things Fall Apart* (1958), selling twenty million copies, translated into fifty-seven languages, and followed by a host of additional works of fiction and nonfiction.

Africa semper aliquid novi

> Pliny the Elder, *Naturalis Historia, Natural History*, ed. and trans. H. Rackman (Cambridge: Harvard University Press, 1940), VIII: xviii, 32-33.

Ngũgĩ wa Thiong'o in Eritrea

Page 75

wa Thiong'o, Ngũgĩ

(1938-). Born and raised in Kenya, major author with lasting creative achievements in a wide range of genre – and in two languages, English and Gĩkũyũ – including novels, plays, short stories, essays and scholarship, criticism, children's literature, and memoir, and whose writings from the early 1960's to the present are frequently reprinted.

Eritrea

Nation in northeastern Africa or the Horn, bordering the Red Sea and newly independent in 1993 after a thirty-year war with Ethiopia.

Gĩkũyũ

Also called Kikuyu; Bantu language spoken by the largest ethnic group in Kenya.

Kiswahili

Also called Swahili; Bantu language of the Swahili people and of eastern and southeastern Africa, where it is also a national language of the Democratic Republic of the Congo, Kenya, Tanzania, and Uganda.

orature

Verbal expression that is artful as literature but only spoken and not written.

Belew Kelew

A pre-Axumite stele in southern Eritrea near the town of Senafe.

Page 76

"Against All Odds"

A seven-day international conference and festival held in Asmara, Eritrea, January 11-17, 2000.

Heinemann
> Publisher founded in London by William Heinemann in 1890 with a long history of corporate changes and with many distinguished authors and series, including the African Writers Series, begun in 1957.

Europhone
> Referring to European languages, spoken and written.

Ertra
> Romanized, alternative spelling of "Eritrea" and pronunciation favored by in-country Eritreans.

Yohannes, Zemhret
> (1956-). Longtime cultural and political leader and author in Eritrea, veteran of the ELF (Eritrean Liberation Front) and the EPLF (Eritrean People's Liberation Front), stalwart of the Peoples Front for Democracy and Justice (PFDJ), and driving force of Eritrea's Research and Documentation Center.

Checole, Kassahun
> (1947-). Born in Eritrea, cultural activist, president, and publisher of Africa World Press and Red Sea Press, begun respectively in 1983 and 1985 and world-renowned for a multitude of books that focus on African, African American, and African diaspora subjects.

Quale guerra
> Italian, "what war?"

Asmara
> Also Asmera, capital of Eritrea, on a site first settled in 800 BCE at an elevation over 7500 feet, and notable, among other things, for its Modernist or Deco architecture built during the Italian occupation in the early decades of the 20th century.

Massawa
> Ancient and pre-Axumite port city of Eritrea on the Red Sea and with a long list of colonial occupiers in addition to being

East Africa's largest and safest port from the 1880s to the 1930s as well as serving as an active port today.

Page 77

The president

Isaias Afewerki (1946-), the first and current president of Eritrea.

Kenya's president

Former Kenyan president (1978-2002), Daniel Arap Moi (1924-2020), who as Kenya's Minister for Home Affairs signed an order on December 29, 1977, for Ngũgĩ wa Thiong'o's detention in a maximum security prison.

Meroë

Ancient capital of the Meroitic kingdom or Kush from ca. 800 to 350 BCE that is now in Sudan.

Aksum

Ancient kingdom in northern Ethiopia and Eritrea from ca. 80 BCE to ca. 825 CE and continuing city, Axum, with a church that claims to house the Ark of the Covenant.

Adulis

Ancient port city near Massawa and at different times through history under the jurisdiction of ancient Egypt, Greece, and Byzantium as well as Hebrew, Christian, and Muslim authorities.

Sahos

Ancient Kushitic ethnic group living in the Horn of Africa.

stele

An ancient monument usually made of stone in the shape of a large panel or pinnacle with inscription and / or drawing(s).

Page 78

Sabean

Ancient ethnic group from Southern Arabia that might go back to 1000 BCE and who had their own, eponymous language and form of writing.

Ge'ez

Ancient, Semitic language and script originating in the region of Ethiopia and Eritrea and no longer spoken today except in Orthodox liturgy.

Segeneyti

Small and picturesque, historic town in southern Eritrea known for its giant sycamore trees.

NGO

Nongovernmental organization usually nonprofit, voluntary, and international, whose projects contend to benefit social, political, medical, and economic development.

Page 80

Ngaahika Ndeenda (I Will Marry When I Want)

1977 play by Ngũgĩ wa Thiong'o and Ngũgĩ wa Mĩriĩ, written and developed for the Kamĩrĩthũ Educational and Cultural Center in central Kenya, and both controversial and influential in its devastating critique of Kenyan government neocolonialism.

Cinema Asmara

Alternative name for the Teatro Asmara, built in Asmara, Eritrea in 1918 for opera performance and designed by the Italian architect, Odoardo Cacagnari, with Romanesque and neoclassical motifs and ceiling painting by Saverio Fresa.

Tigrinya

Widely spoken Semitic language in Eritrea and northern Ethiopia and, like the Tigre and Amharic languages, related Ge'ez.

Tesfai, Alemseged

(1944-). Eritrea's premier contemporary historian, veteran of Eritrean revolution, and prolific author, including pioneering accounts of the history of modern Eritrea, and also drama, translation, fiction, nonfiction, and children's literature.

Mau Mau

Uprising and rebellion in Kenya from 1952-1960 against British colonialism and occupation and, although violent, even more violently suppressed and defeated, yet herald of Kenyan independence in 1963.

Mes tabarhāni 'emer'o

Tigrinya translation by Alemseged Tesfai in 1999 of *I Will Marry When I Want* by Ngũgĩ wa Thiong'o and Ngũgĩ wa Mirii: *Ngaahika Ndeenda* in the original Gĩkũyũ.

Page 81

Papa Susso

(1947-). Distinguished, storied, and well-traveled Gambian griot who plays kora and who has a long family history of griots who have played and constructed koras for centuries.

kora

West African 21-string instrument that is held upright and constructed from a large calabash covered with cow skin and side rivets from which extends a hardwood neck that is smooth and fretless, either catgut or nylon strings, and a bridge.

Sbrit

Longstanding troupe of dancers and musicians who play a variety of instruments and perform indigenous arts of Eritrea's nine ethnic groups nationally and internationally.

nakfa
> The unit of Eritrea's currency and named after the Eritrean town where freedom fighters won their first major victory in the armed struggle for independence.

Page 82

dactylic hexameter
> A line of poetry with six syllables that is dominated by dactyls.

prosodic
> Relating to prosody, the formal, metrical, rhythmic, and technical structure of poetry.

Minor Origins: Adulis

Page 83

DNA
> A double helix molecule in all organisms that contains a genetic code to live and reproduce.

seasonal rivers
> Rivers that are only occasional and not permanent and that form and flow during a rainy season.

Page 84

alabaster
> Fine stone that is white, translucent, and amenable to carving and sculpting.

obsidian
> Volcanic lava rapidly cooled into a kind of black glass-like stone.

malachite
> Fine stone that is green, intensely when crystal, dully when non-crystal, and that can be ornamentally carved.

lapis lazuli
   Semi-precious, uniquely and eponymously blue stone used
   in jewelry, ornamentation, sculpture, and pottery.

platinum
   Chemical element and white metal that is rarer, harder, and
   heavier than gold.

burlap
   Roughly woven hemp or jute that is coarse, thick, and
   protective.

Acknowledgements

"The Woodstock Sandal," *Popular Music and Society*, 43:2, Spring 2020, 146-57, 2020.   https://doi.org/10.1080/03007766.2019.1687674.

"Edgar Allan Poe in Richmond," *Poe and Place*, ed. Philip Phillips (New York: Palgrave Macmillan, 2017), xli-xlvii.

"Gateway," *Jalada* 07:   *After + Life*, 2019, https://jaladaafrica.org/2019/06/01/gateway-by-charles-cantalupo/.

"Domicile," *Per Contra* 34, Winter 2014, http://www.percontra.net/issues/34/poetry/domicile/.

"On a Tree," *The Southern Review*, 52.4, Fall 2016, 642-44.

"Africa Antetranslation" (prose essay), *Research in African Literatures*, 47.3, 1-17.

"Ngũgĩ in Eritrea," *Ngũgĩ: Reflections on his Life of Writing*, ed. Simon Gikandi and Ndirangu Wachanga (Rochester: James Currey, 2018), 36-40.

The author acknowledges support from The Pennsylvania State University, including the College of Liberal Arts and University College. Additional gratitude goes to the Research and

Documentation Center of the State of Eritrea. Thanking Aldon Lynn Nielsen for his "Foreword," the author is one of many who continually benefit from his inspiration, generosity, and comprehensive understanding of poetry. Appreciation for the photographs of Dave Glass, Stephen Greenblatt, Barry Z Levine, Baron Wolman, Joe Sia, and Lawrence Sykes extends literally beyond words. The Beinecke Rare Book and Manuscript Library of Yale University, Christopher Semtner and the Edgar Allan Poe Museum, Creative Commons, Yegizaw Michael, and Abraham Zerai are gratefully acknowledged. The author appreciates the San Francisco Art Exchange and The Museum at Bethel Woods Center for the Arts for their resources and encouragement. Gratitude must be expressed to the book's editors, Girma Demeke and Dawid Kahts, and its designer, Ashraful Haque. Alicia Kiah Cantalupo is thanked for her artwork. Thanks include friends with whom the author went to the Woodstock festival in the first place: Kenneth Abeles, Richard Dorfman, Steven Goodkind, Mark Sisselman, Peggy Wood, and Karen Young. The author deeply appreciates the publisher, Kassahun Checole, who first had the idea for this book and has guided its development. As always, being with Barbara every step of the way is cause for thanks and for celebration.